# DOGS AND GOALS TRAINING VS BEHAVIOR

## HOW TO TRAIN YOUR DOG TO BE ON THE BEST BEHAVIOR

### ALEX GREY

# CONTENTS

# INTRODUCTION

"Dogs do speak, but only to those who know how to listen."
— Orhan Pamuk

Dogs talk to us every day, but are we open to hearing what they have to say? There's more to dog training than teaching your dog to obey commands.

Dogs can be many things to people. They can be protection, family members, comfort, law enforcers, babysitters, and more. When you bring a dog home, more often than not they become a solid unit of the family. This means that there will be a shift in the family dynamic.

The purpose of this guide is to help you fit your dog into your family dynamic. You want your dog to feel at home, but you also want them to meld seamlessly with the family. That can be tricky to accomplish if you've never trained a dog before. There are many misconceptions that exist regarding having a well-behaved and well-trained dog. Many owners hope that if their dog knows a lot of tricks and commands, it makes them well-behaved. Unfortunately, that is not necessarily true. This guide seeks to bridge that gap and help you learn how to take care of your dog in all sorts of situations, from emergencies to their daily care. It will also help you know the right ways to train your dog so that they are safe to be around, for both your current family members and the rest of society.

You might be asking yourself, "What role should I have in training my dog?" and that can be a tricky question to answer when you aren't sure how to read your dog's body language. All dogs will have their own traits and behaviors. Like humans, each dog is different from another. You will find that breeds tend to share certain traits, but inherently each animal will act differently than the last.

Each furry companion will need to be trained so that their behavior is what society expects. For example, the last thing you want is for your dog to bark uncontrollably at all hours of the day, or jump up on your house guests that are visiting you in your home. Going on a walk with your companion can be a nightmare if they run up to or jump up on every person that they encounter. You also don't want to have your companion running around and biting smaller dogs, or attacking people. There are various other undesirable behaviors that you will need to teach your dog are not okay to exhibit.

Whether you have a brand-new puppy, a rescue dog, or an older dog, they can always stand to learn something new. The saying *old dogs can't learn new tricks* doesn't fly with this guide!

Dog training has become a part of society's expectations. All the bad behaviors I mentioned earlier, like barking, jumping up on people, and aggressive behavior, falls on the owner's shoulders. Your dog's behavior becomes the responsibility of the owner. When a dog is well-trained, it makes you a responsible member of society; you're protecting other people as well as the dog. If a dog hurts someone, it becomes a bad situation for the dog and owner alike. Training your furry animal is a necessity if you want them to interact well with those around them, their family, and other strangers they might encounter. There are so many obstacles that can get in the way of your pet adjusting to their new home, and that is why this guide is tailored to help you combat all of them!

Here's another great benefit from training: the bond is only strengthened with your companion. If you're constantly trying to correct a dog's negative behavior, it can be a source of great stress for both owner and companion. However, when you train together, positive outcomes help bring best friends closer together. When you take a personal approach with training a furry companion, it is easier to be in-tune with their signals and their needs. You will get to learn what the animal's body language is communicating, and you can then react appropriately to a companion's needs. I started this introduction explaining that dogs talk to us all the time; training is an opportunity to learn their language.

A trained dog is well-behaved in social situations. This means that when your dog is interacting with other people and other animals, they can get a more positive experience from it because they know how to handle it. An animal that is aggressive or antisocial will miss out on socialization, which can also lead to a host of problems later on.

Trips and vacations happen all the time, and unfortunately, it's not possible to always take our furry friends along for the ride. In these instances, you will need someone to come to the home and look after them, or there may be a need to board them in an unfamiliar place. This can be extremely stressful on a dog that has received no training. When you train your animal companions to react appropriately in social situations, you take away their stress in times when you can't be there to look after them.

Depending on the area a person lives in and the type of training they decide on, dog training can cost a lot of money. Group classes for training can cost anywhere from $30 a class to over $100. It's even more costly if you get private, one-on-one lessons for your pooch. And even after the professional training, the job's not done. You still have to go home and keep training your puppy yourself. So, why not learn the tips and tricks that are needed to get a well-trained dog?

As you read through the different chapters in this book, your understanding of a companion animal will grow deeper. There will be instruction on what behaviors and body language cues your companion is giving you, how to manage their negative behaviors, and how to reinforce positive behavior.

There are basic commands that everyone has heard of like 'sit' and 'stay.' This guide will empower an owner to execute those commands when they train their dog. Don't worry, I won't leave you high and dry on the execution of these training techniques. I will also give instructions on the different methods that can be used to train a dog. Remember, they all have their own personalities, and this means that one method won't work on every dog. Sometimes it is a matter that will need a bit of trial and error. Valuable techniques will be imparted to both the trainer and animal companion. You will teach your animal to follow your commands, and you will also learn how to properly socialize a dog. House-training and potty training will become a breeze following the training in this guide.

The medical care and treatment for your pet can be scary and overwhelming, especially if a veterinarian starts throwing out names of medications and vaccines that you've never heard of before. To help with understanding a pet's vet visits, this guide will review which vaccines are necessary, and what you need to know for your pet's vet visits.You will also learn more about how a reward and punishment system can affect your dog's behaviors, and how to successfully implement a reward system using treats.

Everyone's goals for their dog training will look different, there will be mistakes made and setbacks that need to be corrected. No matter what the ultimate goals are, this guide will help any new trainer accomplish them. It will also give you a list of common mistakes that are made with dog training, and what a trainer can do to avoid them.

There is no need to fear your dog and their bad behavior anymore. Now, the ordinary owner can step into the driver's seat when it comes to teaching their companion right from wrong and good behavior from bad behavior. So, what are you waiting for?

Happy training!

# CHAPTER 1

# CONSIDERATIONS FOR YOUR DOG

Adopting a dog and bringing them home should be part of the final steps. Your first steps should be considering what it really means to expand your family and then doing the necessary research.

Thankfully, I'd love to make life easier when it comes to this step. That's why I devised this chapter to help owners make the right decisions when bringing home a future companion! As we delve into this chapter, the focus is going to be about your dog and how to plan for them, in your budget and home! There's a lot more to adopting a dog than simply bringing one home. You also want to make sure they are loved and cared for, and that's what this chapter is all about.

## Owning a Dog

Choosing to take care of another sentient being can be a huge responsibility, and it's not a decision to take lightly. A lot of thought goes into adding a new member into the family unit — even if they are four-legged furry creatures.

One of the first questions you should ask yourself is, "Am I ready for a puppy?"

It's important to do research into the type of puppy or dog that will join the home. Each breed has different personality traits that can influence how they need to be handled. You want to know what might happen to the family unit before adding another member to the family.

For example, can your finances handle it? The ability to provide for and care for a potential companion should be one of the first considerations. Depending on the size of your dog, the cost of their care can vary annually, from $420 for a small dog to up to $780 for a large dog. This is a rough estimate based on the vaccines, food, vet care, and other supplies they'll need. The type of breed that you adopt can be a big factor in your expenses. Remember, that the costs to bring home a new dog will always be higher in the beginning because there will be a need to buy supplies and get them ready for a new home. So, factor this into any budget if you're about to bring a new member home.

The other aspect to consider is time. Do you get an older rescue or a brand-new puppy? Puppies tend to be a lot more time-consuming as they need a lot of training, a more frequent feeding schedule and time to adapt and bond to their new family.

Puppies are adorable. In fact, it's hard to say no when they're staring at you with wide eyes. However, they are also time-consuming. Puppies need to be fed at least 3 or 4 times throughout the day. Think of them like toddlers that need constant attention and food. They need to eat more frequently so that their bodies can get all the nutrients they need to grow into dogs.

Older rescue dogs take up less time, unless they have some health issues that need a lot of attention. The amount of time and energy that you have to give to a companion should be considered before getting one.

This leads me to my next point. Energy! Depending on the breed you adopt into the family, the level of energy the dog has can vary. Some breeds are very active and require a lot of exercise and physical activity while other breeds are content to sit on your lap and wind down with a good movie and a glass of wine. It's important to do research into what kind of traits a potential pet should have. You want the dog's energy level to match your own.

Consider the size of your home and the space that you have to dedicate to a new pooch. A large dog won't be as comfortable in a small apartment or tiny home. If your space is smaller, then look at different breeds that will fit in with your home and lifestyle.

Dogs are like babies — they're messy. So, think about the time you'll put into cleaning up after a companion. Don't think of it as a negative, animal companions can bring so much joy and laughter to our lives! It is important, however, to be mindful of what cleaning up could look like. For example, a long-haired dog might need more brushing out, or there could be a need to vacuum more frequently. If the furry friend isn't already a part of your life, take into consideration the type of cleaning and grooming that have to take place to keep things neat and tidy.

The most important thing that you can do, for yourself and a future companion, is to do the necessary research. If your heart is set on a particular dog breed, or you've found a rescue is a perfect match, then it will only benefit the owner and dog to understand that breed. Each breed has certain requirements that can be specific, and it's wise to clue your-self in on what these are because you want to provide the best home to a dog.

Ultimately, adding a dog to the home is a big decision. It's not something you commit to for a few days or years, and then pass the torch onto someone else. A dog becomes a member of the family unit, and they do get attached to their people. You'll probably notice that there is one specific person in the home they attach themselves to the most. It's a commitment that lasts a companions' lifetime. So, consider the situation and your ability to take care of a dog in the long term.

When it's time to make the jump into getting a new furry family member, you'll want to know exactly what's needed to spoil them and show care. They can make life very rewarding; of course you want to reward them for all the joy they bring!

## DOG SUPPLIES YOU WILL NEED (AND WANT)

As you start to puppy-proof or dog-proof your home, you'll realize there are a few supplies that are needed. So, what are some of these supplies? Before I delve into an in-depth explanation of the supplies, I'll give you a list. This will get you familiar with the products and names.

- Adjustable dog collar
- ID Tags
- Rabies Vaccine Tags
- Leash
- Dishes for dog's food and water
- Dog toothbrush and toothpaste kit
- Dog crate
- Grooming kit
- Dog bed
- Toys
- Canine Shampoo and Conditioner
- Plastic or metal carrier for transportation
- Scrub brush
- Puppy or dog pads
- Non-toxic enzyme cleaner

- Poop scooper
- Plastic poop bags
- Baby gates
- First aid supplies
- Different types of treats

Some of these items are very self-explanatory, but a few of them require a little more explanation. It's important to understand *why* some items are important and the role that they play in your dog's health and care.

## 1 — Adjustable Dog Collar and Tags

Dog collars are a part of every responsible owner's supply stock. Why? Well, for two main reasons. One of the biggest reasons is that, if your companion gets out or gets lost, a collar helps other people know that he has a home. It separates them from the strays. The other reason is that it makes it easy to attach a leash to your dog for responsible walks and play.

When you get a collar, you want to keep size in mind. If you adopt your companion from puppy age, the odds are that you'll have to buy a size or two up as they grow older. The rule of thumb is to always make sure that you can fit 2 fingers between the dog's neck and the collar. If there is no space to place fingers between their collar, then loosen it or get a new collar.

A collar is also useful for storing a dog's information on it. This brings me to the ID tag which is an essential supply for your animal — especially those that turn out to be escape artists! An ID tag is customizable so you can include a dog's name, a phone number, and even their address. It's up to you what information is put on a tag, but it can be useful when it comes to finding a lost dog.

The other vital tag is the rabies tag This can also attach to their collar. This way, it's easily identifiable that they are up-to-date on their rabies vaccination.

## 2 — Leash

A leash will be necessary for all walks. There are many parks that allow dogs to run unleashed in certain areas and give freedom to play fetch and other games. A leash makes sure that a dog is safe from running into danger, and that people who are walking or jogging are safe as well. It prevents unnecessary accidents from happening until you reach an appropriate place to let your dog run loose.

When you buy a leash, it needs to be between 4-6 feet in length. There are different kinds of leashes that can be bought, such as retractable leashes or old-fashioned leashes. It depends on what works best for you and your pet.

Leashes can attach to a collar or a harness. While a collar and leash are essential dog supplies, you might want a harness instead. A harness is great for more boisterous dogs, as it gives more control over their body without putting a strain on the neck by tugging on the collar.

## 3 — Food Bowls

The best bowls for your pet will be made from steel, glass, or ceramic. The reason for this is that dogs love to chew, and if you get plastic bowls, the odds are that they won't last very long. You want durable food bowls that are also easy to clean. Some dogs can also get acne from plastic bowls and it can be troublesome to fix.

Consider a dog's breed when investing in food bowls. Some breeds with pushed-in faces like French Bulldogs, require a special bowl that makes eating easier on them and their respiratory systems. Other dogs, like golden retrievers, will be fine with a simple stainless-steel bowl.

## 4 — Toothpaste

While it's not essential for many owners, I consider it a life-saver to have a toothbrush and toothpaste for your furry companion. There are special brushes and doggy toothpaste that you can buy at most pet stores or veterinarian offices for your pooch. Never use your own toothpaste for your dogs, as human toothpaste is not good for them or their digestive systems.

Brushing a dog's teeth not only keeps their teeth and gums healthy, it also familiarizes you on a deeper level with your dog. You will know what their mouth, gums, and teeth are supposed to look like. This makes it easier to identify a potential problem before it gets bigger.

## 5 — Crates

Crate training is vital. Especially when bringing home a new puppy, you'll want a crate for them. A growing puppy needs a crate with room to grow. There are large ones available with dividers that help make the space bigger or smaller depending on the dog's needs. A dog crate can be especially useful for rambunctious dogs, and for owners who have to spend large chunks of time away at work.

. . .

## 6 — Grooming Kits

All dogs need to be groomed. Having a grooming kit with a brush or comb on hand, can be extremely useful. Even short-haired pets benefit from being brushed. It's also a great time to bond with your companion, as many of them love the attention that they get when groomed by their owner. However, there are some animals who resent the comb and would rather run wild in the mud. For these dogs, you might want to keep your local groomer's number on speed dial!

## 7 — Toys

A variety of toys is necessary to keep your furry friend happy and productive. These can be:

- Squeaky toys
- Plush toys
- Chew toys
- Treat dispenser

Chew toys are good teaching moments for a new pet. Young puppies use them to teethe, as well. It also helps a trainer redirect bad behavior from chewing on furniture or shoes, to chewing on their toys.

## 8 — Training Devices

There are a variety of items needed to help you train a dog as well. These are:

- Clickers
- Treat pouch
- Bark collars

- Electric collars
- Calming aids

Clickers are the number one tool used in dog training and you will want to add this to your list of must-haves! As we delve deeper into this guide I will go more in-depth about the controversy of electric collars and the practicality of using clickers during training.

I focus on positive reinforcement and the clicker is an essential tool for that, so get one to maximize your success with your companion.

If you have a skittish dog, calming aids such as calming treats or thunder-jackets can help them during times of high anxiety. For example, a dog that is scared of thunder can benefit from a thunder-jacket. These are tight-fitting jackets that press around the companion to give them a sense of security. Think of it like a security blanket.

*Ultimately, it will be easier to train your dog and instill good behavior in them, if they feel like your home is their home. They need to be welcomed into the environment you are providing. More importantly, they need to feel safe.*

# GETTING YOUR HOME
# READY

There is a lot that goes into getting a home ready for a new companion. It's not as easy as adopting a dog and bringing him home. If you already have a dog in your home, then I am sure that you're familiar with the dirt that these lovable companions can track in and out of the home. There's also a penchant for getting their noses into things that they really shouldn't. It's up to the owner to make sure that the pet is safe from things that can harm them and from things you don't want them to destroy. One of the best ways to do this is to prepare a space in the home that is specifically for your dog. There are several ways to do this.

*The first is to dedicate a pet room for them. If there is space, then a dog will benefit from having their own room for eating, sleeping, and playing. It helps to limit the mess they make to that one area, and makes cleaning up a lot easier. A pet room is never complete without a plush and comfortable bed, their own food bowls, and toys! Get as creative as you want and make the entire room pet-themed.*

Not all owners have that luxury, or even want to create a separate room for their companions. I find that a nook or corner for your pet can do the same job as a room. Plus, some dogs like being in the center of the family. Your creativity is your only limit with a nook for your dog. You can build this in any corner, under stairs, or in any area that suits you and fits your dog's needs. I love pet nooks, and I'll try to keep my dog's nook close to a window. This gives them some outside stimulation, because they get to see nature.

Another way to prep the home for your new companion is to get dog gates — also known as baby gates. This is especially helpful to section off areas of the house that you don't want your dog sticking their nose into. Doggy gates can protect your home and also protect your pet. There might be rooms like a laundry room that you don't want your companion getting into, and these can help prevent incidents from happening. There is a vast array of gate styles, so you can easily find one that matches both your needs and your home style.

Having their own space will help them feel safe and important — particularly when their favorite bed and toys accompany the space that you give them.

What about pet-proofing your place? It's not the same as baby-proofing, as our lovable companions often find ways to dig their noses into danger more frequently than our babies do. Pet-proofing is as important as making sure you have all the necessary supplies.

If you've already brought your dog home you can still take steps to make sure that the house is safe for your pooch. Keep this checklist with you when running through your home:

- Ensure that all trash is tucked away and bin lids are secure.

- Lock all cabinets and drawers that you don't want
  your dog to get into.
- Set up gates and close doors to rooms and areas not
  meant for your dog.
- Make sure that electrical cords are covered or
  hidden out of sight.
- Keep your bags out of reach.
- Have all medications locked away and out of reach
  of sniffing noses.
- Put poisonous plants away, or remove them from
  the house.
- Create their own space for them.
- Set rules and enforce them.
- Pack away all batteries and other small chewable
  items that your dog can get into.

Don't give your dog access to counters and other high surfaces, they should stay on the ground

Does that seem like a lot? There's a lot to do when it comes to getting your home ready for your companion, but it doesn't have to be overwhelming.

My best advice is to start room by room. Tackle a little at a time if you can. In a worst-case scenario, buy the doggy gates and set them up, slowly opening a room for your dog once you have dog-proofed it and started their training.

It's important you make sure that you've kept toxic items out of your dog's reach. These include all plants that could be potentially harmful, plastic bags, cleaners, and strong chemicals, garden insecticides, mothballs, laundry detergent, and many other chemicals that can harm their sensitive systems. Keeping these items out of reach is also the best way to avoid an expensive vet bill and unnecessary pain for your puppy. Dogs don't always know what they can and can't eat, this is where preparation comes into play.

Making sure that these are out of your companion's reach can be as easy as adding a tight seal cap to the chemicals, or placing a seal on the cabinet that stores them. Again, you could section off rooms with doggy doors that you don't want your dog accessing. You might consider moving all chemicals up high. This way, they are out of reach for your dog who stays low on the ground.

As your dog gets comfortable in your home, you'll find that they enjoy smaller areas and spaces. Open and large spaces can be intimidating — especially to a new puppy in a new home. Let them familiarize themselves with one room. This allows them to feel safe, and if they get spooked, then they have a safe haven to run back to.


## Where Should They Stay?

Dogs aren't meant to live outside. You should never leave your dog outside in a yard where they are at the behest of the elements. Having a safe space inside the home is imperative for them.

A dog crate can come in handy because you can keep it in a centralized area that is best for the family and the dog. Since it is also a smaller space, it can become a safe space for your dog when they feel scared or uncertain. It can limit the mess they make if they choose to sleep in and play in their crate.

If you have to leave the home and can't take the dog with, placing them in a dog crate is the best thing for them and for the home. You shouldn't leave a dog unsupervised in the home unless they are well-trained and have shown themselves to be trustworthy. Even then, there are chances that the dog can find their nose into something they shouldn't.

When you set up your dog's crate, try to keep it in a central area, so they feel close to the family, but be aware of how noisy the area is. If your dog is trying to sleep, a noise-filled area won't be conducive to their rest. Puppies and older dogs sleep a lot and need their rest.

Like humans, dogs get cold and hot. So, if you leave them outside among the elements, they won't do well. Keeping them inside means that they experience the same temperature control that you do. If you're too hot or too cold, then the odds are that your pet is feeling the same way.

Creating a space in your home and enforcing rules is a part of training your dog. It could be a new puppy or it could be a dog that has been in the family for years and there will be negative behavioral issues. This all stems from a lack of proper training. When you know how to train a companion, the family benefits from their good behavior. You want to be able to leave the dog at home while on an errand run. To do that, you want to start with training basics. Remember, every aspect of dog care ties into training.

**Can My Pet Eat Anything?**

Dog diets are specific. There are some foods that we enjoy that can be really detrimental to your dog's health. As much as your new companion might have you believe they can eat whatever you're eating, this isn't always the case. It's up to you to know what is good for your new family member.

Some breeds have more sensitive stomachs than others, and this means that they require specialized diets. Human food

— even the smallest amount — can upset their stomachs. It's always best to be cautious and get to know your dog before feeding them things that aren't a part of their natural diet.

General food items that you should avoid feeding all dogs are:

- Avocado
- Chocolate (The methylxanthine substances in chocolate can cause diarrhea, vomiting, heavy panting, tremors, seizures, thirst, frequent urination, and in extreme cases death.)
- Coffee and other caffeine products
- Alcohol (I feel like this one goes without saying, but alcohol can cause massive heart failure, vomiting, comas, seizures and even death in dogs.)
- Citrus fruits
- Grapes (Can cause kidney failure in dogs - raisins should be avoided too.)
- Macadamia nuts and oils (This is an absolute no! These nuts can cause your dog to go into hypothermia, and experience depression, bone weakness, vomiting, and tremors. The symptoms will appear between 12 and 24 hours after the macadamia has been ingested and will last for days. It's best to avoid other nuts as well.)
- Garlic
- Raw foods such as meat, eggs and even bones (These foods can contain harmful bacteria like E. coli and salmonella. You might wonder about bones, and yes, dogs in the wild would eat bones. However, domesticated dogs are at risk for injury when eating bones. They could choke or get

splinters in their digestive tract. It's best to not feed
them bones if you can help it. If you do, watch your
pet carefully and make sure it's not a bone that
easily splinters.)

- Xylitol (A sweetener that is often used in low-
calorie foods, can cause liver failure in dogs.)

When feeding your dog, try to stick to your veterinary recommended diet. Make sure that their bowls are always clean and that you replenish their water daily. If you do like to share food from your plate with your dog, make sure that your food doesn't constitute more than 10 percent of their overall diet.

Puppies will have different food requirements than older dogs. Since puppies are still growing and maturing, they need more vitamins and a higher number of calories than older dogs do.

If you're unsure of how much to feed a dog, consult a veterinarian on their specific needs. Food measurements will vary based on the dog's breed, size, and weight. Most bags of food give a measurement on the side to let you know how much to feed a dog.

Switching dog foods can be tricky, but sometimes it is necessary. Unless the vet recommends that you stop a particular make immediately, never stop an old diet cold-turkey. Try your best to blend in their new diet and slowly phase out the old diet. It should take a minimum of 7 days and a maximum of 14 days to switch a dog's diet. Try your best not to change their diets up a lot, because this can cause upset stomachs.

You can feed a dog either all canned or all dried food. If you prefer to mix it up, that can work too. I like to feed my dogs the canned food as a treat. If you have a picky eater, canned food is often the way to their hearts. Keep in mind though that dry food will lead to more solid stool from a dog that is easier to clean up.

The AAFCO (Association of American Feed Control Officials) will include dietary information for dogs on the bags of food that are bought. This can help guide a feeding schedule. Typically, adult dogs get fed once or twice in a day, but if their needs vary, you might find yourself adapting this to best suit your schedule and companion.

# GROOMING

Before you try to groom your dog at home, I recommend that you work on your training first. A well-trained and well-behaved dog will be easier to groom than an unruly one. Dogs can sure have a lot of opinions when it comes to you trimming their claws.

Grooming can lead to a bunch of questions from owners. When do I do it? What if they hate it? How often should I groom them? What does grooming entail?

The answer is — it depends entirely on your dog. Some dogs won't be able to be groomed at home — especially without training. In this case, you can take them to the vet or the local groomers to have their baths or their nails done.

However, if you can, grooming at home is a great way to bond with your companion and to learn more about your dog's health. Who else can be a better expert on your dog than you, when you take care of all their needs?

When you groom your dog at home, it deepens the relationship that you have built. Some dogs might take time to adapt to a new at-home grooming schedule, but once it is part of their routine, it is beneficial for both pet and owner.

## First Tip — You Need Trust

After working on training, my first tip is to make sure that there is a solid foundation of trust when you attempt to groom your dog. Very few dogs will patiently sit while a stranger gropes them, brushes them, and takes clippers to their nails. You don't want to get hurt, and you don't want to hurt the dog. If your dog trusts you, then you're a step ahead of the grooming game.

## Second Tip — Develop a Routine

Before you start grooming, figure out a routine that will work for you and the pooch, and do your best to stick to it. When they know the routine and what's coming, the pet will more than likely fall in line behind you, because they trust your process.

You'll need a few things to get into the grooming groove:

- A comb
- Brush or shedding blade (you can find these on Amazon or at your local pet store)
- A grooming table if necessary - you can also use a mat to place your dog on to groom them
- Grooming shears
- Grooming clippers, you will use a #10 blade so that you don't nick their skin
- Nail clipper/nail grinder
- Styptic powder - in case you hit the nail's quick and need to stop a bleed

Most grooming kits will be outfitted with all the tools needed, so do your research and buy the one that is best for the dog. For example, for a short-haired dog, the odds of needing hair clippers won't be very high, but you'll still need a brush and nail clipper.

Remember to practice patience as you start the grooming process. Your dog will feed off your vibes. If you're calm, cool and collected, the odds are that they will be too.

Try not to let times between grooming get too far apart. Set a regular schedule and stick to it. The pet will love the routine, and hair and nails don't get unruly. All the items used to groom a dog should be made for dogs and pets. Other products could become unsafe and injure the pet if they're not made for them. Also, never handle your pet in the dark. This could lead to injury to the owner and pet. Choose a well-lit area, and try to groom during the day if possible.

Sometimes, there's only so much you can do. Always know your limits and the dog's limits. Don't push them into doing something that they clearly don't want to do. And don't try to force their hands. If it's not happening, and it's more a fight than anything, stand back and let go. There are professional groomers for this reason.

**Brushing and Bathing**

When you're introducing your dog to brushing, start out slow. Do it a couple of times each week and only for a few minutes, unless they really love it and want to be brushed all the time. If you maintain regular brushing, you can make your grooming days easier — especially for those long-haired pooches.

Bathing is great occasionally, but brushing is going to be your best friend. Even before a bath, you should brush your dog out. This helps to get the top layer of dirt off, and also to shed them of excess hair that can later get matted.

If your dog has long hair, look at combs and brushes for long-haired dogs. You can also try a metal pin brush, which will help you pull out that dirt that gets entangled in their fur. A dog that is brushed before a bath leaves cleaner water, which makes a cleaner dog.

Bathing your dog should be done when they're extremely dirty (think "my dog just nose-dived into fresh mud") or smelly. When you bathe your dog, always do it on a warm day and avoid using blow dryers to dry them off. A towel will be your best friend. Some dogs can get terrified of the loud sounds, like blowing air from the hairdryer, and this can lead them to have a negative feeling about being groomed.

**Clipping Your Dog's Hair**

Once the dog is brushed out, washed, and dried;, you might think about clipping away some hair. Always make sure that you use the right kinds of clippers or scissors for the pet. If it's not made for dogs — don't use it. If you have a long-haired dog and grooming them is a ritual, try investing in a grooming table. This way you can secure the dog to the table and make sure they get the best cut.

Never cut your dog's hair while it is wet. You want your dog to be dry and clean before you do anything to their fur.

**Pro-tip:** When trimming the hair on a dog's paws, only use the tips of your scissors. The same goes for their facial area and tail area. This can prevent a bad cut from happening to your dog if they jerk or move suddenly. If you need to trim ear hair, always hold the tips of the ear with your fingers. This lets you know where the ear stops and the hair starts.

Matted fur should always be sheared off with clippers. Never use scissors as you can cut their delicate skin.

**Shaving Your Dog**

Be careful with shaving. You need a sharp blade on your clippers to do this, but always use a #10 blade so you don't risk cutting them. When you shave your companion, make sure that there are no distractions around for them or you.

The first place to start is by their neck, and then slowly move the clippers down your dog's body. Your blade should be angled flat along their skin. Take extra precaution when you are shaving around their delicate skin, such as their thighs and hips.

Never use anything other than a #10 blade on your dog's face and sensitive areas. These are delicate areas that can get cut if a different blade is used.

<u>Pro-tip:</u> always double-check the heat on the machine and the blade. If the blade gets too hot while you're using it, you risk burning their skin.

If at any time you feel unsure of yourself when it comes to shaving your dog, skip this step. Let a professional handle it.

**Nail Trims**

Some dogs are great about nail trims, and others only get them when the professionals do them.

If you want to use a nail grinder on your dog, try acclimating them to the sound first. This will help them feel more at ease when you trim their nails, because it won't be a foreign noise.

It's easier to see the quick of a dog's nails if their claws are white. Where the pink part of their nail starts is considered the quick. You want to avoid nicking the quick at all costs. If your dog's nails are black it can be a little trickier. Gently clip their nails away, until all you see is a black dot that's solid at the tip of their nails. That's where their quick starts.

As much as you might want to, avoid clipping their nails slowly. A slow clip or a dull blade can make the nail split. Occasionally, clipping the quick might happen. This is where it is useful to have styptic powder on hand ahead of time, to stop any bleeding.

**More Grooming Tips**

When you groom your best friend, always check their ears and clean them if necessary. Most stores and vets sell an ear cleaning solution that can help you do this.

Run your hands through the pet's coat and look through it. You don't want to miss out on fleas and ticks. It's also important that the dog has tick and flea prevention on and up to date. For example, Revolution is a great brand for fleas and ticks as well as worms. You put it on once a month, and they're protected! There are other brands to look at too.

Each breed will have different grooming needs. Animals With long fur or double coats will require more care and grooming than those who are short-haired. Research and time with a dog will help identify exactly what they need.

Try not to rush the process of grooming. Take your time to make sure it's done right and that the dog is loving it. At the end of the day, it can take trial and error!

# CHAPTER 2

# FUNDAMENTALS OF TRAINING

Without a foundation, houses sink and crack. The same goes for dog training. In order to do it effectively, you need a strong foundation. Watching someone else teach your dog the fundamentals, doesn't help you learn the basics that you need to know to keep training at home.

Training and learning for dogs doesn't stop when they get out of obedience school. They're constantly learning, and you're always teaching them. As we sift through the material in this chapter, each section will make up a layer of your foundation in dog training.

## Well-Trained Vs. Well-Behaved

There is a common misconception between well-trained and well-behaved. A dog can be well-trained and yet, still misbehave.

My dog Bailey was first brought home as a puppy. She was about three months old when I brought her home. As a

French Bulldog she had a rambunctious and playful personality, but also enjoyed a good snooze.

For the longest time I would brag to my friends about how well-behaved Bailey was. After all, she had done her obedience school, and I had diligently completed her training at home.

Bailey responded to sit, roll over, high five, stay, heel, and come. She even ran when her name was called. However, I soon began to notice a pattern. Bailey only ever listened when there was an incentive.

Whenever I called her name, it was a choice whether to listen to me and come or not. The times she came? Well, those were all treat driven. When I shook the bag of treats, called her name and told her to sit, Bailey was only too happy to perform for a tasty treat.

One day, I had a friend come over to my house for lunch. I had told her all about how well-behaved Bailey was, and she was eager to meet the new puppy. Well, this great behavior lasted five seconds until Bailey decided that jumping on my friend and chewing at her heels was a great way to get attention. I was appalled. My friend laughed it off. I got the trusty bag of treats, and soon enough, Bailey was back to doing her commands and sitting and heeling.

My dog was well-trained, not well-behaved. In fact, it became obvious to me through the course of lunch, that Bailey had a lot to work on when it came to good behavior. She ran around the table, barked at birds and squirrels outside, and even begged for scraps of food as we ate. I had always thought that, because she listened to my commands, she was well-behaved, but this lunch hour had me realizing that her behavior was far from good.

Here's the thing. Your dog can know every trick in the book and follow the tricks perfectly in order to get a treat, but this doesn't mean that the dog is well-behaved. Their only mission is to do what they've been trained to do in order to be rewarded. The animal has learned that you expect a certain behavior from them to get reward. This is why dog behaviorists are so important in the dog industry. Any person can train a dog to sit for a treat. That's actually the easy part.

The hard part is understanding your dog's behaviors and learning how to change them from ill-mannered to well-behaved. This will require you to not only understand your dog, but to also form a strong connection with the animal. Each dog is going to learn differently, and knowing yours can help you learn the best ways to teach them.

Before training begins, the concept and distinction between well-behaved and well-trained needs to be understood. A well-trained dog will heel when you're calling it and get a treat, but a well-behaved dog will avoid jumping on your house guests, because it knows that is bad behavior. A well-behaved dog is always a priority over a well-trained dog.

Luckily for us, we don't have to choose between the two. Through understanding your animal and employing the right training techniques, you can have a dog that is both well-trained and well-behaved. All you need is the knowledge and to practice your training skills.

When it comes to training your companion, consistency is key. Practice it every chance you get and at every opportunity. Remember that if an animal is exhibiting behavioral issues, training it to sit and heel won't change these behavioral issues. Basic obedience lessons and training are not a cure for misbehavior.

Training is important, don't misunderstand me. However, in order to have a well-trained dog, you really want to focus on well-behaved first.

**Why Rehabilitation is Important**

Rehabilitation of your companion's behaviors can be especially important if you've adopted a dog that is older or rescued a stray. These older dogs can come with bad behaviors and learned traits that they experienced in their old homes, and that you don't want them to continue with. This can be very difficult to do, but the payoff is definitely worth it!

Your dog is going to look up to you as a guide. This means that the responsibility to teach them the difference between the right behavior and wrong behavior, will fall on your shoulders. Whether old dog or new puppy, there is so much for them to learn when they merge into your family unit, and it's important you lay the rules and boundaries out from the very beginning.

The top things you want to work on first with your new companion will be:

- Listening and respecting you
- Potty training
- Crate training
- Walking on a leash
- Interacting with other dogs and people the right way

With rehabilitation, you are seeking to change the animal's way of understanding and interacting with their world around them. It is used to improve the dog's quality of life as well as the quality of home life.

Whenever your dog displays negative behaviors that you do not want them to exhibit, it's important that you start rehabilitating them and end the behavior instantly. Nipping negative behaviors in the bud, the first chance you get, can stop negative patterns from being created.

For example, lots of owners allow their puppies to take part in negative behaviors because they think it's cute, and that they will grow out of it the older they get. For instance, when Bailey started jumping on my lunch guest. It's cute when they're puppies, slightly annoying, but cute. It's not so cute when they're older dogs or bigger dogs and can seriously hurt someone by jumping up and down.

The truth is that puppies won't grow out of negative patterns you allow to happen. They need to be taught what's inappropriate when it happens. If you allow them to keep up a negative behavior, it will be a lot harder to correct along the way.

Think of it this way: Your purpose with dog training is to get your companion to obey a command that you give it. There are many different types of training that take place, however, the most common type is positive reinforcement — or rewards-based training. Positive reinforcement works best with rehabilitating older dogs because it gives them a positive reward and reason to change existing behaviors.

Dog training however, doesn't solve those pesky behavioral issues we've talked about. In these instances, you want to shift your focus from training to rehabilitation. It sounds scary, but it's simply a more apt way to describe correcting bad behavior in your dog.

## How to Start Rehabilitation

Before you can start on rehabilitation, you need to examine your dog's environment. What's new? What's different? What's setting off their negative behaviors? Then, look at your dog and how they interact with their environment. Is your companion bored? Are they getting overstimulated? Are they afraid of something?

Asking yourself these questions can help you find the crux of the problem faster. Don't underestimate your own feelings and energy in relation to your dog. Animals pick up on moods and energies, and if you or someone in their environment displays negative energy, that can affect your dog's behavior. If you remain calm and assertive when training them, they'll respond with calm.

Changing their environment can make rehabilitation easier for you. It's also critical that you understand the different types of training techniques so that you can rehabilitate your companion. If you don't know how to train them or what method to use then there won't be a successful elimination of negative behaviors.

# REWARDS VS PUNISHMENT-BASED TRAINING

For a sure you've heard of rewards-based training. It's the idea of giving your companion a treat once they have successfully completed a behavior or trick that you deem appropriate.

There are other techniques that were once vastly popular, but are now being phased out. Punishment-based training used to be at the forefront of training dogs. However, there's a reason it's fading into the background. Punishment-based training involves the use of scaring and hurting a dog to incentivize them to perform in the way that the trainer wants the dog to perform. They can scold, yell, pull on the leash, and an array of other negative reinforcements.

Punishment-based training makes the ultimate goal to stop or reduce your dog from perpetrating a behavior.

Rewards-based training employs positive measures and reinforcements. This can occur in the form of treats, verbal praise, and giving the dog a toy. The point of positive reinforcement like rewards-based training is to get your dog to increase or continue a good behavior.

A study was conducted that researched the way 364 people trained their dogs (Fratt, 2004).

The goal was to see if the way a dog was trained had an impact on their behavior. They also wanted to see which model for training produced the best results.

When they surveyed the trainers, the results came back that a total of:

- 12 percent of people used physical punishment to train
- 66 percent of people used vocal punishment to train
- 60 percent of people used positive praise
- 51 percent of people used treats and food incentives as rewards
- 11 percent of people used a toy or playtime as rewards

Keep in mind that this study was conducted in 2004. This was around the time that punishment-based training was starting to be seen for the bad guy it really is. After the researchers surveyed training tactics, they then had the trainers rate their dog's obedience. The results were staggering. Those who used positive reinforcements had higher levels of obedience and compliance in their dogs than those who used punishment-based training.Part of the reason that dogs trained through the punishment method behave less is because they have developed anxious personalities.

At the end of the day, the way you train your animal ties into your care for the animal. In the past, punishment methods were traditionally used. However, there is research that stems all the way back to 1997, that highlight and prove the negative traits that dogs develop as a result of punishment-based training.

Even if you choose not to personally train your dog from start to finish, and you seek the aid of a dog training facility, it is vital to know what kind of training they will impart on your dog. Especially since you will have to carry the training out at home as well. This will help you make sure that your trainer is teaching your dog in ways that you agree with.

**Negative Ways that Dogs are Impacted**

Some of the negative ways that dogs are impacted through punishment-based training are:

- suffering and pain
- various health risks that stem from increased levels of stress

When the 2004 study was conducted, it showed that out of those surveyed, 20 percent of trainers and owners used rewards-based training. 10 percent of those surveyed used punishment-based training, and 60 percent used a combination of rewards and punishment-based training. A further 10 percent declined to mention their training methods.(Fratt, 2004).

Despite the proof that rewards-based training is the best for the dog, there are still a few people out there who believe that punishment-based training is more effective. However, in the survey, it was found that dogs that were trained using punishment scored lower each time, than those dogs who were trained using rewards. The point of rewards-based training is to increase desired behavior in your dog. As you see in the study, dogs that were given a chew toy to replace an inappropriate item, gave up the inappropriate item and chewed on the toy. Those dogs who were punished went back to the original item later on.

**Tips on how to train and not to train**

Dogs won't remember hours later why they are being punished or corrected. When undesirable behavior is seen, it's imperative that it is corrected in the moment. Then move on. Don't make the correction the biggest part of the issue. When correcting their behavior without fuss, your dog is far more likely to listen. The correction shouldn't hurt your dog, or make them afraid of you or the consequences.

Training your dog won't necessarily be a walk in the park. But there's a few things needed to keep in mind when working with your companion.

As you would parent a child, think about parenting a dog that way. Don't focus on their negative behaviors, but instead highlight their good behavior. Always be kind and gentle with them when you are correcting them and training them. Dogs will respond to your energy.

Aggression won't stop aggressive behavior in a dog. In fact, it's likely to worsen the animal's aggression. As I mentioned above, a dog will feed off of your energy. If you're angry and aggressive, then that is the same energy the companion will show back.

When training a dog, it's never helpful to be physically violent against them. Don't roll their bodies, jab them, angrily stare at, and even pin them down to get them to do what you want them to do. If you have a foundation of trust with your companion and you're building a bond, then they will start to slowly listen and obey if you stay consistent with training. There's never a need to physically hurt them to get them to listen.

Whether training or not, be aware of interactions with your furry friend. Try your best to have fun and pleasant interactions with the animal. When training, remember to take breaks and play with the dog. This allows them to bond with you as well, in a non-training way.

Keep in mind that when a dog does something you see as undesirable, they won't remember it in the future. Feelings like guilt and shame don't stay with them hours and days after they've done something you see as negative behavior. Never continue to punish them for days for something they did in the past. They will fail to understand why you're punishing them.

When training a companion, look out for signs of boredom and stress. Signs can vary from subtle indications such as yawning and looking away from you to obvious signs like growling and biting. When the animal starts to exhibit stress and anxiety during training moments, take a step back and analyze your behavior, then their behavior. Don't continue to try to train. Take a break. Play with the companion if they'll let you, or give them some space. Remember, dogs have feelings and moods too. Dogs won't always do exactly what we want when we want.

# CHAPTER 3

# TRAINING TECHNIQUES

There are many different methods to use when training a dog or puppy. Some of them overlap into one another. You will find the method that works for your companion. Keep in mind that what works for one dog might not work for another. In this section, we're going to explore the most common training methods. You can scratch some of these methods from your training regimen, you can use more than one method at a time, or you can diligently focus on only one type of technique. It's entirely up to you which method you find more successful.

## Positive Reinforcement

Training methods that use only positive reinforcement (rewards-based training) have quickly surged in the last two decades. Especially after a high-profile trainer successfully used it on former president Barack Obama's dog.

## What is Positive Reinforcement?

This training method runs off of the theory that, if a dog is rewarded for good behavior, it will repeat this. All bad behavior is not met with a reward. However, this method takes it one step further than not treating bad conduct. You don't acknowledge the dog's bad deportment.

If a dog needs to be corrected, you'll remove the reward, which is their toy or treat, instead. You never punish your dog physically or verbally with this technique.

## How to Execute Positive Reinforcement

As your pet performs behavior that you want, reward them instantly. Don't wait an hour or two, within seconds of your dog performing the desired action, you should hand them their treat. Dogs don't remember like we do, so if you give them the reward immediately they'll be more likely to connect their action to the treat.

Through this training technique, remain regular and consistent. If you have more than one member in the household, ensure that everyone uses this method of training. The commands and rewards should be uniform for everyone interacting with the dog.

## Tips for Moving Forward with Training

So, how do you exactly wean them off the rewards? At first, reward the dog every single time they exhibit the desired action. As your dog becomes more consistent in displaying the appropriate behavior, you will then only reward them occasionally for the action, not every time.

Be cautious to not give your dog a reward for bad behavior or negative behavior. For example, I had a friend that I was helping to train her puppy. She had a rambunctious border collie, and it needed a little guidance. Every time her puppy would bark at the squirrels and neighborhood cats, she would open the door and let the puppy out. This is seen as a reward to the dog. They are being taught that barking will get the door open, and they'll be able to play outside. You have to be consistent in your own behavior and not reward their bad behavior. If you ignore it, and they see they will not get rewarded for barking, then this behavior will stop.

My biggest tip_is in regard to using treats as rewards. Use small treats. You don't want to overfeed your pet, as you want to maintain their weight. Smaller treats will prevent overfeeding them as they get rewarded for good behavior.

Commands will be learned very quickly through this training technique. However, I implore you to practice patience if you are correcting undesired behavior. It will take time for your companion to make the connection between the desired behavior and the treat.

## Clicker Training

You have probably heard of clicker training at some point. It can be used as a stand-alone method, but it also pairs well with positive, reinforcement-based training. The foundation of these two training methods cross paths often. It's a way of conditioning your animal's behavior.

## What is Clicker Training?

Clicker training uses a device that emits a simple noise. Usually, it is a whistle, a sharp noise, or even a clicker. With this device, you make the sound as soon as the dog has completed the desired behavior that you want. Through this method, your companion will learn exactly when they've completed the behavior that you want to see. They'll know why you're giving them a reward and what it was for. As the dog adjusts to the clicker training, you can shift from the clicker, to training and creating desired behaviors with your verbal commands, like "sit" and "heel."

**How to Clicker Train**

At first, you'll need to condition the dog to recognize that at the sound of the whistle or click, they'll be rewarded. After this, they'll begin to learn that certain behaviors will earn them a click and that leads to a reward. As they learn that, then you can implement verbal commands. This will help them make the connection with the click and the verbal commands, so they know what you are asking them to do.

The first step in clicker training is getting your dog used to the sound and what it means. We call the noise of the clicker the marker. To do this, simply click your clicker and immediately follow it up with a treat. Repeat this between 15 and 25 times. This will help a dog rapidly learn that the sound of the marker means a reward is coming. Once they have this behavior down, you can move onto clicker training with commands.

**Tips for Clicker Training**

It's a great foundation for teaching your dog tricks and for helping them understand more intricate commands. Clicker training is also a fantastic way to shape a dog's behavior. If you're having dinner and you see your dog peacefully laying in their bed, click and reward them for this action. It's teaching them that not begging is the desired behavior. Use the marker to reward them for behavior that you want to see, even if an active training session is not going on.

Clicker training, on its own, doesn't necessarily help with training away undesired habits. However, pairing it with other techniques can help you produce a well-rounded dog, in both behavior and trained tricks.

## Scientific Training

This training technique is a little more complicated to explain than its counterparts. Science is always changing and evolving. So, the foundation for this training is constantly shifting as well.

### What is Scientific Training?

The purpose of scientific training is to attempt to understand your dog's instincts and natural behavior. You also want to understand how easily they can be conditioned, and how effective the rewards vs punishment systems are in relation to training.

Our understanding of a dog's psychology is always shifting, as new studies are constantly bringing in new information that we didn't know before. Through this technique, if you want to correct or change a behavior, you should first understand the behavior.

You might notice that certain beliefs and practices from the scientific training technique are used and employed in other techniques as well. So, the information learned from this technique has several other applications.

. . .

## How to Use Scientific Training

Through this method, you'll be doing a lot of research on a dog's psychology and behaviors. You'll also have to be up-to-date on the latest studies performed on dogs. Instead of rewarding a dog for every good behavior, this technique tries to blend in both a reward and punishment system.

Scientific Training is largely based on two concepts known as operant conditioning and classical conditioning that work together to help train an animal.

When you are using classical conditioning the goal is to teach a dog associations with commands that are verbal and nonverbal. So, you want your dog to know that phrases like "walk time" means they will get to go outside.

Operant conditioning aims to teach the dog that their behavior has consequences. This means, your dog learns that the set of actions they display can lead to variable outcomes. For example, a sitting dog gets a treat, but a jumping dog gets ignored. This teaches the dog to choose their behavior to receive a desirable outcome.

So, when you use these methods, it melds together a positive and a negative consequence.

## Tips for Scientific Training

Scientific training doesn't rely on an equal, rewards vs punishment system. It uses punishment sparingly, but also doesn't reward a dog every time they do something desired.

As you explore this avenue of training, one of the key aspects is to examine your dog's environment and find out what they respond to. These are the reinforcers. Reinforcers can be treats, food, toys, attention, and other variables that strengthen the behavior you want your dog to emit.

This method of training requires an understanding of why your animal is exhibiting a certain behavior. That's why research and getting a personal understanding of your companion is so important.

## Mirror Training

Mirror training can also be called the model-rival method of training. The premise of this training is based on the idea that dogs learn by watching. So, the idea is, if you offer a model that displays the desired behavior, then your dog will mirror that behavior.

Alternatively, it's also known as the model-rival method because you can use a rival for resources to help the dog learn and copy the behaviors you want them to exhibit.

## How to Mirror Train

A model can be anything you want. Another dog can be used, but the most common practice is to use a person to be your model or rival. The dog will watch you praise or punish the model for certain behavior. As the dog observes, it will learn what to do and what not to do, based on the trainer's reactions.

If you use the human as a rival, you can have them compete with the dog to gain a reward. This has also been shown to fast track a dog's ability to pick up on the task or behavior you want them to exhibit.

Mirror training will more closely fall into the model part of the method, because you are using the human model as a mirror for the dog's behavior. It's a great way to show that dogs can learn by example. Many trainers use this method, as they find it comes more naturally to them and their dogs than other techniques.

For example, if you use another human as the model, you can have them sit and then reward that behavior. The dog will see that their model got a treat, and they will attempt to mirror the behavior in an effort to receive a reward as well.


### Tips for the Mirror Method

The stronger your bond and level of trust with your dog, the more they will mirror your energy and behavior. So, you need to remember that you are the mirror to your dog as well.

Mirror training doesn't stop on the training field. When you are home in a personal space, the owner becomes the dog's model. Remember to watch how you respond to them and other environmental stimuli as your companion will be learning from these actions.


### Electric Training

This technique employs the use of the electric collar. The electric collar can do one of two things. It can either shock the dog, or spray citronella by their face. The shock or spray only happens when the dog is exhibiting undesired behavior, or not listening to a command.


### How to Train with Electric Training

Sometimes a leash cannot be used on your dog, so in those instances, the collar will be used for distance training. The most common way this is used is to teach dogs to stay in the boundaries of their yards. The collar will shock the dog for wandering outside boundaries.

Before you place any type of electric collar on your companion, make sure that the animal understands basic commands such as "sit" and "stay."

Conditioning the dog to the collar is the second step of training. Let the animal get used to the idea of the collar. Put it on them every morning and when going on walks so that the dog doesn't perceive the collar in a negative light. Keep the power on the collar off unless you and the dog are in an active training session. In this way, it won't become a feared object.

During training, you might tighten the collar by one notch. Normally, the collar needs to be touching the dog's skin to work (remember that you still need two fingers between skin and collar even when training). Also, keep training sessions short using a collar because you can quickly frustrate a dog.

Don't seek to give the dog pain. The collar should merely be an annoyance to them like a mosquito buzzing in your ear is an annoyance to you.

So, when training you start with the collar on and you use it as a form of annoyance to the dog. When they start to obey the command, then you turn off the electric collar. This teaches the dog that when they obey a command, the annoyance goes away.

**Tips and Cautionary Note about Electric Training**

While there are those who praise the use of electric collars and say they are better than choke collars, it's still a training method that uses punishment to correct behavior. Your dog will only learn the behavior that they should not exhibit through this technique. It doesn't teach them the behavior that you want to see.

Never attempt to turn the stimulation on the collar above the level of annoyance. Causing your dog pain can create a mass of behavioral issues and aggressive behavior that is hard to correct down the line.

Keep in mind that these devices and this kind of technique can lead to higher levels of stress in your dog and cause major anxiety problems. If you're not experienced with training or dogs, I suggest you ignore this method completely, because you risk overusing it and hurting your dogs physically and mentally.

## Alpha-Dog Training/Dominance Training

I am sure that you have heard of being the alpha dog before. This method makes use of the natural instinct dogs possess. There is a pack-like mentality in dogs that makes them create a relationship of alpha and submissive.

## What is Dominance Training?

This method is based on the theory that a dog will view their family as their pack, therefore, there will be a hierarchy to follow. The same is true of wolf packs in the wild. If a dog believes they are the alpha, then they won't respect their humans or your commands. They'll try to dominate you.

If they see you as the alpha, the idea is that they will submit. It is critical to learn and understand your dog's body language when making use of this technique. When you project confidence, your dog will be more likely to listen to your authority. It is demonstrated through simple things like eating first, entering a room first, leaving a room first, or controlling leashed walks.

## How to Dominance Train

One way the alpha-dog method is used to train, is to make sure that your dog is obeying and submissive before engaging in a behavior. For example, if you're going to take your dog out for a walk, then you'll want your dog to be seated and waiting patiently for you. Until they display this behavior, the door doesn't get opened and there is no walk.

Upon beginning alpha dog training or dominance training you need to be confident. If you are calm and confident, the dog will follow your example.

Remember that the dog is a dog and not a person. They will have a different way of viewing the world and this is imperative to understand. As training starts, commands should be simple. Never repeat yourself. Your dog should listen the first time or it calls into question the trainer's position as alpha.

## Tips for Dominance Training

Alpha-training methods can be hard on some families because some family members may have difficulty being alpha. The dog needs to submit to you, and you need to be seen as a top dog. This means that your dog doesn't get on the couches or your bed to lie down and cuddle. You also can't get down on the ground to their eye level and play with them.

If you do that, then you are signaling to your dog that they are your equal. The entire technique is based on you remaining dominant and in charge. Keep in mind that not all research supports this method. Some research states that dogs don't view their family members in the same way they might view their pack in the wild.

This method can help you stop your dog from displaying undesirable behavior, but it doesn't get to the root cause of your dog's behavior. It can also make your dog feel fearful of you. A side note to remember, is that this method can't be let up. It always needs reinforcement. If you have children around this method can become dangerous for them to be around.

## Desensitization

This technique is where you recreate a situation for your dog and see how they behave. You control the level of the stimulus so that you can heighten your dog's level of success each time. It is particularly useful when you are trying to help your dog overcome a fear or negative behavior. However, you do need to be careful not to overwhelm your dog with the stimulus. If you begin to overwhelm your dog when you recreate a situation you want them to solve or experience, then they will only learn to be overwhelmed. This is not your goal.

### How to Desensitize Train

When you begin desensitizing training, your goal is to slowly introduce the object of your dog's fear without scaring them. It's a fine balance and can be tricky to achieve.

Let's use fireworks as an example. Many dogs are terrified of the loud bangs emitted from these beautiful displays of colors, and they can become traumatized. Some companions even end up running away from home in fear.

You don't want to scare your puppy or dog, so using fireworks won't help at the beginning to desensitize them. Try finding a recording of fireworks, it can be a video or a simple audio recording.

The point of desensitization is to get a dog used to a sound, object, or event that used to cause fear. So, when playing the audio of the fireworks, start on a barely audible level — remember that a dog's hearing is far superior to a human's. Slowly, increase the level of the audio over several times of playing it.

If the dog ever shows signs of fear or stress, go back down a notch and start back at the level that they were comfortable with. Keep exposing them to tolerable levels of the object of their fear until they no longer live with fear and stress.

## Counter-Conditioning

This is another technique used to help your dog overcome fear and anxiety. For example, if there is a certain noise that causes fear, then that is the stimulus. A good example is the nail grinder. Many dogs can become fearful of the noise of the nail grinders used to keep their nails trimmed.

## What is Counter-Conditioning?

The object of counter-conditioning is to change their response to the stimulus. You do this by changing their association with the stimulus. Instead of it being fear inducing, you change the stimulus to occur in conjunction with a treat or reward when they see or hear the stimulus. This will make the dog become more conditioned to the stimulus, and see it as a positive rather than something to be fearful of.

## How to Counter-Condition

You want the dog to get accustomed to something they fear or detest. It's really simple when putting the ideas of counter-conditioning into practice, it merely takes repetition and consistency.

Let's say that your dog has a fear of being around other animals. This can become a problem whenever the dog needs to go for a walk or you take them to a park where other animals get a chance to run around and play. Nobody wants their dog to experience stress when interacting with other animals.

The first step will be to reward the dog every time they're exposed to other dogs (or the object of their stress). It can't be any type of treat either. You want them to get over their fear so the idea is to choose a delectable food item that they only receive when met with the stimuli.

Every single time the dog interacts or sees another, give it that special treat. Over time, the dog will learn that good interaction with other animals leads to a treat, and they won't be stressed when going into public situations.

## Top Tips on Counter-Conditioning

The main thing to focus on is consistency. For example, if you're walking your dog, the treat must be given every single time that another dog is seen. It won't work if you intermittently give the treat. It can seem tedious, but the proof is in the pudding!

When first starting with counter-conditioning make sure that it all happens in a controlled environment where you can control the situation and your dog's exposure. This makes it easier and more successful in the long run.

## Response Substitution

With this technique, you will focus on using desirable behaviors to replace undesirable behavior. Reinforced rewards and detracting focus are the main methods used to complement this method.

It takes a lot of time and practice to get this technique right. It's easiest if you don't let your dog participate in negative behaviors. If you know a certain situation will lead to bad behavior, avoid it.

## How to Train Response Substitution

Response substitution is one of the trickier training techniques. I always advise owners to lean on a behavioral therapist if this is the route they choose to take.

With response substitution you can employ both desensitization techniques and counter-conditioning techniques, because they go hand in hand with one another. If a dog is already accustomed to positive reinforcement training, it can make response substitution easier because they already have a foundation of understanding that desired behavior leads to a reward.

First, create an environment that you can control. The idea is to change a response, so there will need to be an area free of distraction that you can slowly expose the dog to the stimuli that is creating the negative behavior. With the use of rewards, treat the companion when they have shown the desired behavior. Don't reward them if they half-complete a behavior.

The key here is to slowly introduce the stimuli. You can't expose them to levels that cause fear and expect the dog to respond in an appropriate manner. Building a foundation slowly is the correct way to handle this training.

In cases of aggressive behavior, always bring in a trained behaviorist trainer so that they can assist you and ensure that the environment is safe for humans and animals.

## Relationship-Based Training

Relationship-based training is one of the most popular training methods because of its success, and its incorporation of other techniques to make up one all-encompassing training method.

While it does use other techniques in its method, the main focus on this type of training is the individual relationship between the dog and its owner. This training method can be so personalized to each dog and owner, that it can fit your needs and personality quite easily.

Instead of trying to simply correct the behavior, the goal of relationship-based training is to meet the needs and requirements of both the dog and the trainer. It places an important role on communication between dog and human, and at the end of the day, it can greatly strengthen a bond.

This relationship should always be mutually beneficial to both animal and human. An owner must familiarize themselves with a dog's body language — and then more specifically their own dog's body language.

A bond between you and your dog will require necessary insight into understanding their body language, to know what treats and rewards motivate them best, and to make sure that all their needs are met.

There is a focus on positive reinforcement with this training style because research has overwhelmingly shown that positive reinforcement is the best way to achieve desired behavior from your companion.

There will be a need to limit and control your dog's environment and their outside stimulus. This helps ensure that unwanted behavior doesn't occur and is corrected when it does.

When training actively, you want to control your dog's environment. If they don't know how to obey your commands in a quiet area, they won't learn it in a busy park or with a ton of distractions in the backyard. As your dog shows that they are becoming more proficient in the commands and tasks, then you can slowly increase the level of difficulty. Add in a distraction or two to see how they handle it. Don't increase the difficulty until the dog has shown that they've mastered each level.

Punishment isn't used in this scenario because it can damage your relationship with your companion. Instead, if your dog misbehaves or doesn't complete a command, then it lies on you to find out why. Ask yourself these questions:

- Could the dog hear me?
- Were there too many distractions?
- Is the dog hurt?
- Are his needs met?

This type of training will help you bond with your dog, but it doesn't happen overnight. Time and patience will be your best friend as you navigate the training field.

You've probably already noticed that relationship-based training uses a lot of other techniques to form this one method of training. It makes use of what works, and has been shown to be successful with other methods, to give you the best chance of success at training your dog.

Instead of relying on what you want, this method also requires that you think and feel about your dog's emotions and point of view. What do they want? How are they feeling? All of this prompts a greater bond between pet and owner.

It's similar to raising babies to toddlers and then to young children. You can only give them the tools to set themselves up for success and then continue to train and build on top of that success; at the same time working on your relationship with them. Dogs are a lot like children.

As we delve deeper into training, there will be a distinct focus on relationship-based training and how to incorporate it.

# CHAPTER 4

# RELATIONSHIP-BASED TRAINING

As I'm sure you've realized by now, I believe that the best form of training for your dog is to base it around relationship-based training. The focus of the previous chapter was to give you a rudimentary understanding of dog training so that you could begin to form your foundation. As you understand the concepts and grasp the basics of training, it's time to start building a house on top of that foundation.

We all want our dogs to be well-behaved and well-trained, and this is one of the most successful and effective ways to achieve those goals. We are slowly building on the fundamentals and imparting you with the knowledge you need to know before you try training your dog.

The first thing is to earn your dog's respect. Because respect means they will want to spend time with you, and they'll be more open to receiving instruction.

Before thinking about starting relationship-based training, remove all ideas of punishment from the mind. Any physical harm or verbal harm that is brought upon your dog will only damage the relationship instead of build it up. Negative techniques like that are never used with this type of training.

The biggest benefit that I find from relationship-based training, is that it both teaches new behavior and corrects current misbehavior.

Through this process there will be continual reinforcement and support of the type of behavior that the companion should exhibit. This starts the animal off on the right foot and leads them to a successful training session. Remember, old dogs can learn new tricks so don't hesitate starting this type of training on older companions you might already have, or an older rescue animal that was adopted.

Here's the thing when it comes to this type of training. All your interactions with your dog are going to be a learning experience for them. This can even be extended beyond your formal training sessions. Even if you don't mean to, you are training them when you speak to them, play with them, and interact in other ways with them. This type of training follows you and flows into your lifestyle, because it creates constant communication with your dog.

Other methods focus on a given command and the dog's ability to execute them. This type of training works both ways, not merely an owner giving a command. It is beneficial because it means there will always be the opportunity to show a companion the behaviors that they are expected to exhibit. You'll be able to easily reinforce their positive behaviors because learning never stops.

As you know by now, this method focuses on the relationship and bond that is formed between an owner and their companion. How exactly can this be done? How can you enter into a training session that benefits both owner and companion?

**Relationship-Based Training Tips**

The first thing you need to do is to give priority to your dog's needs. Your desires and needs come second. Make sure that your pet is taken care of and feeling great before you start training. A quick list of things to check is:

- Are they hurt or sick?
- Are they afraid of me?
- Are they afraid of something else?
- Are they frustrated?
- Do they need to eat?
- Do they need to drink water?
- Do they need to go potty?
- Have they gotten enough exercise today?
- Are they tired?

If you can identify any need of an animal that is lacking, then that need should be attended to before training. An animal that is feeling good will be more receptive to training methods. If they're tired or frustrated, the training session can be detrimental to both owner and dog.

When you get your dog, it's important that you start learning their body language and what they're trying to communicate to you. Many myths have colored society's understanding of dogs, impacting an owner's idea of their dog's body language. Misconceptions can cause a negative impact on the relationship with a dog because of this lack of understanding. Throw out preconceived ideas of being an alpha and needing to dominate the pack. The dog won't see you that way.

The best way to understand and learn a dog's body language is to be up to date on the research regarding a dog's body language. Do the research on your specific breed of dog. Be empowered and armed with the right information when training a companion. This is where science-based techniques come into play. A dog has a way of talking to those around them. Ninety percent of communication between humans is non-verbal. So it stands to reason a lot of non-verbal communication happens between an owner and dog. They let you know if they're happy, sad, angry, frustrated, and a wide range of other feelings. When you start to understand what they're telling you, then communication flows better.

It helps to know what best motivates them when training begins. All dogs are different. Some prefer affection while others want treats or toys. And yet, some dogs do great with simple verbal praises. When you discover what their secret is, use their preferred reward to help with training.

Our animals don't always fall in love with us immediately. It takes time to build a relationship with them. Spending time with your dog before trying to train them can help you solidify a bond that will make them more likely to work with you in training. If you spend time with your dog, make sure they're encouraged through positive reinforcements. This makes the dog look forward to time spent with you.

Under positive reinforcement there are some techniques that you can use to heighten your chances of success at redirecting and reinforcing good behaviors. They are capturing, luring, shaping, and cueing.

1. **Capturing** is when you use verbal praise and treats to get your dog to repeat good behavior that they've done on the spot. This behavior isn't necessarily driven behind a command. For example, you see the dog sit on its own, and you praise it, saying, "Good sit, good sit. Sit." They learn quickly to connect the word to the behavior. Capturing takes time and consistency, but it is so simple that even younger family members can participate! Start by arming yourself with a bag of treats. You can also use a clicker to help signify when the dog has completed the desired action. Whenever the dog performs the desired action, click or vocalize to signal they've done it and reward them. A word of caution is to never interrupt the behavior with the reward. For example, if your dog is coming towards you don't reward them with a treat that might stop their behavior. Wait for the animal to follow through with the desired behavior and then reward them.

2. **Luring** is when you use a treat or reward to grab the dog's focus and attention. You then use the treat and slowly move it around to see if the dog responds by following it with their eyes, head, or whole body. You can use this to put their bodies in the correct posture you want them to be in, or to have them perform a behavior you want them to repeat. When you first start training with luring, use a treat to guide the dog into the desired movement and behavior. Have the dog follow the treat about 10-15 times. Once the behavior is successful, phase out the treat by using non-verbal cues. If the treat isn't phased out then there is a risk that the companion will only obey the command when they follow a treat. You don't want to risk this. This is a great method of training for new trainers because it is simple and effective. Once the dog is obeying the non-verbal commands without

the treat, move into using verbal commands with intermittent treats to lure them into the behavior. Eventually, phase out all treats and have them obey the command only.

**3. Shaping** is when you reward any behavior that is close to the behavior that you have set as a goal for your dog. Slowly, you use the reward to change their behavior to the exact outcome you've desired. While shaping, you will reward minute behaviors that will eventually bring the animal toward the full behavior you want to see. I find shaping particularly successful with crate training. This is what training with shaping will look like: you start by placing the animal near the desired object or behavior. For my example I'm going to use the crate. I would place the crate down and reward the dog for going near it. This teaches them that it is not something to fear. The companion will want more treats, so they will perform the behavior again to get a reward. Make it gradually harder for them to get the treat. Wait until they put a paw into the crate or walk into the crate before they get the next treat. Keep raising the challenge until the dog has successfully completed the behavior. Remember to reward the companion for obeying. Shaping lets the dog work towards the goal at their own pace.

**4. Cueing** takes a behavior that your dog knows and adds a signal to the behavior. For example, if your dog already knows how to sit, cueing will be adding in either a visual or auditory signal to the command. This will teach your dog to obey when they see or hear the signal. It's essential to train a dog their cues, especially if the bulk of their learning came with clicker sounds. A dog that already knows to sit when they hear the click, needs to learn non-verbal and verbal cues for this behavior. The easiest way to train the animal will be to withhold the click until they obey your vocal command. For example, in a training session, use a non-verbal cue to tell your dog to sit. This can be accompanied with a verbal cue as well. Once they have obeyed, hand out the treat with the click. This trains the dog to listen for the cue from the owner instead of the click. To make it more difficult, add multiple cues like "sit" and "come" and "sit" again. Take away the clicker and practice it until they listen to only your cues.

**Never use negative training methods, like punishment, to try to train your dog. Force, pain, fear, intimidation, the threat of injury, and even dominance won't help you eliminate the undesirable behavior your dog takes part in. If your dog is doing something you don't want them to, ignore the behavior or redirect their focus. Replace a negative behavior with a positive one.**

Let's go back to Bailey for a moment. I needed her to understand that jumping on someone wasn't the right way to greet them. I wanted her to be well-behaved, and this meant sitting and staying in place when being introduced to someone new. I started using her favorite treats and giving them to her only when she performed the right behavior. If she jumped up on someone, she was ignored and that was the opposite of what she wanted. Verbal praise also helped direct her to the appropriate behavior.

A big reason why dogs continue to take part in unwanted behavior is because they have the freedom to do so. Control their environment as much as you can. For example, if your dog won't stop barking at the animals passing by the window outside, simply limit their ability to get to the window. Don't allow them to sit there and bark. Put a gate up so that they can't continue to take part in negative behaviors.

Your dog is like a child and will need supervision — especially while in this training phase. You need to supervise them to make sure that they won't perform negative behaviors when you aren't looking. In this way you're setting them up for success. When they don't have the opportunity to practice and perfect unwanted behaviors, it becomes easier to correct if it happens.

When I first brought Bailey home, I watched her all the time. She wasn't potty trained yet, and I didn't want her doing her business all over the house. I isolated her into an area of the house where I could easily watch her and reinforce the behaviors I wanted from her. It helped set us both up for success with her training later on.

Sometimes you'll find that your dog is acting out of emotion. Animals are sentient beings, and so they experience a spectrum of emotions that same way that we do as humans. They can get angry, frustrated, and fearful. The easiest way to correct behavior that stems from emotion is to change what they are feeling. For example, if a certain situation makes your dog afraid, try incorporating something they truly love along with the situation.

Bailey used to be very fearful of the vacuum. She hated when it would come out, and she wouldn't stop barking until it was put away. I realized she was afraid, so to combat her fear I would pass her a toy that she loved, only when the vacuum was out. Fairly soon she was so ready for her toy, she didn't pay the vacuum that much attention.

The more you spend time and train your dog, the easier it will be to learn their habits and their language. Your relationship will help your dog trust your movements and where you are leading them.

I find that when I am training my dog at home, it is best when new behavior or tricks are learned in a quiet area that is free from distractions. This includes other pets and family members. Slowly, as she learns the behavior I want her to perform, I make it a little harder and harder. I add in a distraction here and there, to make sure she understands the basic principle of the behavior I want her to exhibit.

Sometimes you need to go back to step one. Even if you're halfway through training a certain behavior, it can be helpful to go back to the first step if your dog is having issues performing on a more difficult level. Always give your companion constant feedback about their behavior and what they're getting right.

Sometimes you might wonder why your dog isn't listening to your commands. The answer is normally really simply. If you've made sure that their needs are met before you begin training, then you have a few other things that could be preventing your dog from obeying.

If they're distracted, it can cause them to focus on the distraction instead of the command you are given. They might not understand what you're asking them to do. This means you'll simply have to go back to basics, and keep practicing until they understand your command. Taking them to a distraction-free zone can help reinforce the basics. They might not listen to you because they didn't hear what you said. Make sure that you have their attention before you give a command.

If they're scared or you see them get stressed it is best to end training for the day, and attend to their emotional needs.

Sometimes your dog thinks that you giving a command is a choice that they can choose to follow or not. When this happens, make sure that you only give them the command once, and let them follow through. Don't budge on your command. Follow through with the one behavior that you are trying to teach. If you switch the command before the dog completes the first one, it can become confusing.

# BODY LANGUAGE

People that don't think their dogs are talking to them simply aren't paying attention. They have their own way of talking to us, and part of training is starting to understand what they're telling us. The main parts of the body that all dog's use to communicate with are the eyes, mouth, ears, tail, their sweat, and the way they hold and move their bodies.

### Eyes

Let's start with a dog's eyes. The sclera of a dog can tell you a lot about their emotions. The sclera is the white part of their eye. A tense dog will have round eyes and their pupils will dilate as the sclera becomes visible around the eye.

If their pupils are dilated your dog is telling you one of a few things. They can be afraid or they can be aroused. Checking their environment can help you determine what emotion your dog is experiencing.

If your dog's eyes are dilated and glassy, then this is a sign that they are experiencing stress or feeling like there is a threat around.

Squinting eyes are a sign that means that your dog is relaxed. You'll see their eyes change shape into an almond, and the sclera will mostly disappear.

### Mouth

Your dog's mouth can also tell you if they're relaxed or tense. If their mouth is open, and they're lightly panting, then this indicates that your dog is relaxed. Focus on more than if their mouth is open or closed. A relaxed dog could also have the corners of their mouth pointing upwards, as if they are smiling.

A dog that is in a state of fear will have their mouth closed. If they're afraid, they might even start to pull the lips backwards at the corners of their mouth. A faster, rapid panting can let you know if your dog is tense and afraid.

If your dog was relaxed and suddenly snaps his mouth closed, then this is a sign that their environment has changed and added in a stressor. If there is no food to cause your dog to drool and salivate, then drool becomes another sign of overwhelming stress or fear.

Your dog will always warn you and others before it does something. One of the signs a dog gives in warning, is to wrinkle the skin at the top of its muzzle. Once this is done, they might follow the wrinkle up with showing the front of its teeth by pulling their lips up. Occasionally, this could also be backed up with a growl. Many dogs may take this position if a stranger is approaching you. Watch their body language carefully to gauge what your dog is feeling.

You'll also notice that your dog can smile. At least, their canine version of smiling. This is an act of submissiveness. Their lips will be pulled back and up and their teeth will be exposed. However, it's easy to know when they're grinning because their eyes will squint and their tail will be wagging. Sometimes you need to take a look at several different body language traits to identify exactly what your dog is telling you.

Identifying your dog's body language can help you tailor training sessions to get the most from them. If your dog begins to yawn a lot, or they start licking their lips often, it indicates that they're getting stressed.

### Tail

Wagging tails are known throughout the world to be a sign of a happy and content dog. But the tail can tell as a lot more than that. Actually, you want to look at a lot more than if the tail is moving or not. Here are two things to focus on when reading your dog's tail:

- How the tail moves
- What position the base of the tail stays in

If your dog is relaxed then you will see their tail held neutrally. It will simply extend from the spine at or slightly below the level of the spine. A dog that feels excited will have their tail above the level of their spine.

A dog that is afraid will have their tail sharply tucked between their hind legs. Depending on the length of the tail it can also stay stiff against the belly when they are scared.

You might watch your dog's tail gently wag from one side to the other, when they're happy or playing. The more aroused and excited they become, the harder their tail wags. Slow long movements will turn into quick side-to-side wags.

*Ears*

I'm sure you've seen that many breeds are identified by their different types of ears. They're part of what makes a dog so special. Some dogs have ears that make it easy to identify their moods while other dogs give us more of a challenge. The key with this is to focus on the base of your dog's ear.

A relaxed dog will have the base of their ears pulled ever so slightly back, or flopped and resting to the sides. A curious dog, interested, or aroused by something in particular, will have the base of their ears forward and pointed towards the direction of their interest.

*Sweat*

Your dog's sweat can tell you what they're thinking. Panting is what a dog uses to cool their bodies. That's why on a hot summer's day you'll often find your dog in the shade, panting away.

It's crucial to recognize the change in your dog's type of panting. Normally it's slower and relaxed, however, when a dog gets stressed, their panting can increase rapidly. You might notice their mouths tighten and wrinkle as well.

An upset dog sweats a lot. If you notice that your dog is leaving behind wet paw prints on your flooring when walking around, it's a sign that something has upset them (either that or they're tracking mud all over the house!)

*Hair*

When your dog has hair raised on their back, then this could mean they're upset or aroused. It's more commonly known as "raised hackles" in the dog community. Raised hackles aren't strictly relegated to the back, and can happen on your dog's shoulders, right above the base of their tail and all along their spine.

If your dog raises their hackles, it's not an instant sign that they're going to get aggressive, but it does let you know that something is up. Survey their environment to get the full picture and understand what they're telling you.

Sometimes when a dog is extremely scared or experiencing prolonged periods of stress, you will notice that their hair falls out a lot more. If your dog starts shedding more than usual, take a look at their environment and try to identify their stressors.

**Movement and Posture**

Your dog moves a lot throughout the day, and they're definitely telling you how they feel with their movements. However, their posture when they sit and are relaxed also tells you more than you think.

A playful dog or a dog ready to play and be excited, will generally bow its head down with its front paws and have over-excited body movements with excited facial expressions. A playful dog will have a wriggly body, and they'll move around a lot from one foot to another. You might also see them stop briefly and stay still for a moment before starting their exaggerated movements again.

If you, or another dog, are trying to interest a still dog in playing, pay attention to their cues. If they stay still, and they don't move with bounce, they might not be interested in playing. If they move away, then give the dog its space.

If your dog starts to sniff, lie down, look away from you, or starts scratching, then this indicates that they're avoiding you or a particular situation.

Dogs can experience fear on different levels — the same way humans do. If they're a little scared then you might see them tremble. They might follow this up by leaning away or crouching down to make themselves seem smaller. You might also notice that their pupils are wide open.

If your dog becomes terrified, you might see them exhibit the "flight" part of fight or flight. They'll scramble and try to get far away from what's causing the fear. If you bring what they are fearful of closer to them, and they feel truly terrified, they can also defecate.

Aggressive body language is displayed by the dog trying to seem bigger than they are. Their heads will be pushed up above their shoulders. Instead of the loose body you see when they play, their muscles will be rigid and tense. Typically, they'll center their weight, or they could lean forward, bearing their weight on their front paws.

## Eight Feelings Your Dog is Trying to Tell You

As you learn your dog's body posture and movement, you'll notice that there are about eight main things they try to communicate to you.

## Relaxed and Approachable

A dog that feels this way won't feel threatened by their surroundings, and is safe to visit and meet. You'll notice that their ears are up and pointing straight but not forward. They'll have their mouth open and sometimes their tongue might be sticking out. Their posture will be loose, and they won't be tense. You'll also notice that their tail is down and relaxed.

## Alert and Examining

While your dog is alert, they are also assessing what the appropriate action or emotion to display is. An alert dog is characterized by their eyes stretched forward and their mouth closed. Their eyes will be open wide. Their tail will be held up and out, straight in line with their back, but it won't be bristled. They'll also stand on the top of their toes and put their weight on them by leaning forward. In their face, you'll notice that their forehead and nose remain smooth (unless you have a wrinkly faced dog!)

## Fearful and Aggressive

There are two different types of aggressive behavior that your dog can display. When your dog is fearful and aggressive this means that even though they are afraid, they may still attack. Their fearfulness doesn't lend into submission. Generally, your dog will face the person that is making them feel this way, and wrinkle their nose. Their body will also be lowered toward the ground, and they could have raised hackles. You will notice that their tail is tucked between their legs and their ears are pulled back. They will curl their lips and pull their mouth backwards at the corners.

## Dominant and Aggressive

A dominant, aggressive dog will have different body language. You will notice that their tail will be raised and often bristled and bushy. They'll have wrinkles on their head and nose. Their lips will be curled and their teeth visible. Their mouths will be opened and their ears pushed forward. Their body will be tense and their posture will be stiff. An animal that is displaying this behavior is confident in themselves and warning the threat that if they are pushed, they will attack.

## Fearful and Worried

They indicate this by putting their ears back and smoothing their forehead. You might see their tail wag a little bit, but it will still be in the down position. They will lower their body, and will make brief eye contact or just look at the ground. You might even notice them sweat and leave behind wet paw prints.

This position is indicating submission. They're trying to pacify another animal or person. They will also show this by licking at the air or the dominant being, and raising a paw in the air. Your dog is anxious and uncomfortable when they demonstrate this type of body movement and posture.

## Distressed

Their body will be lowered, pupils dilated, and their ears pulled back. You can pick up on their stress because they might be panting very rapidly with their mouth open. Their tail will be down, and they might be sweating (through their paws). The difference in this posture and the other types of fear and aggression, is that when your dog is stressed and distressed, they will not exhibit their feelings toward any one particular person. It's normally something in their environment causing it.

## Extreme Fear

When they do this, they are demonstrating total submission. They are indicating that they know they are not dominant, and they accept that fact. You will see them move onto their back and expose both their stomachs and their throats.

Their ears will be flat and pulled back. You might see them urinate or defecate as well. They'll move their head and avoid direct eye contact with whoever they are afraid of and submitting to.

**Ready to Play!**

An invitation to play is normally highlighted by an open mouth with tongue exposed. They'll have their tail lifted and wagging slightly or quickly, depending on their level of excitement. They might bow down on their front paws as the first invite to play, and then dart off in excitement. Their ears will be up but not pulled forward and their bodies will be loose. You will also notice their pupils get dilated.

**Tie It All Together**

As you can tell, understanding your dog's body language goes hand-in-hand with training. If you don't know what they're trying to tell you, how will you begin to instruct them? How will you respond appropriately to their communication?

Never stray from keeping your relationship with your dog at the center of your training. If you keep asking yourself, "How do I strengthen our bond?" then you will find that understanding their communication is at the top of the answers.

There are some key things you need to offer your dog, in order to deepen that bond. A connection is necessary. Occasionally giving your dog attention, or not being present when you interact with them, won't cut it. Treat your dog like you would if you wanted to be a friend. Seek them out, try to know where they are and what they're doing, and then join in on their fun.

Without empathy there is no relationship. This type of training focuses on an empathetic connection and understanding of your dog's emotions. Try to look at things from your dog's perspective.

# CHAPTER 5
# HOUSE TRAINING

Training! A never-ending cycle of learning. We're continuing to build our house on the foundation that we laid out. Let's put the front door in, as we start to learn about house training our companions.

When you bring home a furry friend, they won't have all the skills they need in order to properly exist in your living space. This is especially true if you are bringing home a puppy.

Your companion will need training, so that they learn where they can make a mess and where they can't. They also need to know what not to chew on, or play with (and break)! This can be a process, so I recommend you grab your trusty friend, patience, and saddle in for the ride.

As we delve into this chapter, we will cover everything from potty training to crate training and even a few of those commands!

## Potty Training

Everyone loves a potty-trained dog or puppy. It makes life so much easier! However, you need to do the work before you can reap the benefits. Potty training can seem like a stressful time for a new dog parent, however, if you keep your relationship with your puppy at the heart of it then it becomes a lot easier to handle.

At the end of the day, training a puppy requires patience and consistency on your part. Use techniques based on positive reinforcement to encourage them along. Teach them the correct behavior and set them up for success. This will deepen the bond and connection you have.

When I tell you to bring your patience, it's because of the time frame it takes to get a puppy properly house-trained. Most puppies can be house-trained between 4 and 6 months. However, every puppy learns differently, and it can take some puppies a year to be house-trained well.

The breed's size comes into play, as well. The smaller the breed, the smaller their bladder. This usually necessitates more trips outside than a bigger breed.

You also want to take into account what your puppy or dog could have experienced in their previous home. Sometimes, you need to put in work to break them of old negative behaviors before teaching them the desired behaviors you want. Remember, it's baby steps, and sometimes you have to go back to the beginning to reach the finish line.

The best time to train your puppy will be when they are around 12 to 16 weeks old. This is when they really gain control of their bowel movements and their bladder. You can train them to hold it in until they're able to eliminate (within reasonable amounts of time). While it is not impossible to train an older puppy or dog, it will require more time than if you started when the puppy was young.

Sometimes you will find that when you bring puppies home from the breeders they have a bad habit of eating their own waste. This is often when they've been stuck in a cage, and they eliminate in the same cage that they sleep in. This will be a behavior that you have to work on correcting first before moving on to proper elimination. Situations like this are where verbal praise and rewards will be your best weapon.

So, how do you start house training that brand-new puppy? Well, let's take a look.

**Steps to Potty Training**

Before you do anything, you'll want to make sure that you've dedicated an area in your home to your puppy. This could be a room, an area of a room, or even a crate. Eventually, your puppy will understand that elimination needs to happen outside. When they begin to understand this concept, then you can allow the puppy to move around the house a little more freely.

It is helpful if you keep your puppy on a stable and consistent feeding schedule. When meals are over, take the food away from your puppy so that they can't free feed. This gives you control over their elimination.

Puppies are young, and so they will go potty often. It's best if you can set aside time when you are home to help teach your puppy elimination methods, but your crate training can become handy in situations where you have to be at work or be away from the home for prolonged periods.

First thing in the morning you should take your puppy outside (use a leash while they are still learning) and let them go potty. After this, set an alarm to take them out every 45 minutes to an hour.

Get into a routine that whenever meal time is over, they get to go outside for a chance to eliminate again.

If your puppy is napping and wakes up, get in the habit of taking them outside to give them a chance to do their business. Before bedtime is a good time to let them out, one last time.

Consistency is key with potty training, so even when you take your puppy outside to do their business, make sure that you take them to the same spot over and over again. The puppy will smell the scent from their previous times going potty, and it will prompt them to go in that same spot again.

Never leave your puppy outside alone, while it is learning. As you are training it, stand with them and watch as they eliminate — well, maybe not watch them do their business, dogs like privacy too.

Staying outside with your puppy is imperative in the training process because it means that you can give verbal praise and rewards, immediately after your puppy eliminates in the right place. Remember that rewards don't always have to be food related. You could give them attention or take them on a short walk outside. It's whatever speaks to your puppy best. When I house-trained Bailey, food was her only motivation. So, I made sure to leave her favorite treats for the behaviors I really wanted her to get down.

Sometimes our schedules don't allow us to take the puppy outside every hour or so. In this case, you will need to get a crate to potty train your puppy. It's a good short-term solution, but it won't work long-term. You still need to actively work on teaching your puppy to eliminate outside when you have the time.

Using the crate will help your puppy learn to hold in their bladder and bowel movements until you let them out for their potty time. However, there are a few rules to follow when using a crate.

- Your crate should be big enough for your puppy or dog to stand in, move their body around, and lay down. However, there should not be enough space for them to eliminate.
- For puppies that need to be in the crate for over two hours, ensure that they have a source of water. Use a water dispenser that attaches to the outside. This way your puppy won't tip over their water bowl.
- Eight hours is too long for your new puppy to be stuck in a crate with no break to go potty. Unfortunately, this is the typical work schedule. While your puppy is still young (so for about the first 8 months), make sure that either you or someone else can give them a break and let them out halfway through the day.
- If the animal starts eliminating in the crate, then stop the use of the crate. It normally is bringing bad behaviors with it from its previous home. Possibly, the crate is too big for the puppy or it isn't getting enough chances to go outside to do their business.

*How to Know When It's Time to Go*

Your puppy will show you several signs when they need to use the restroom. It's up to you to pay attention and recognize these signs.

When confined in an area, and they start to bark and scratch at a door or gate, this is a sign that they need to go outside to potty. Other signs can include whining, moving in a circle, sniffing corners or other areas of the house, and general barking to get your attention.

Sometimes you'll experience setbacks. This is especially true for someone who is still learning the training ropes themselves. Don't berate your puppy for these setbacks. They happen to everyone. There could be a long list of reasons why your companion had an accident in the house, and it can range from not being trained completely, to a change in the dog's environment or lifestyle.

Don't let accidents stop you from training. Stay consistent and stick to your schedule as much as possible. If you're really struggling months later, then it might be time to talk to a veterinarian or a dog behavior specialist to help get you on track and to rule out medical conditions.

## Medical Conditions that Lead to Incontinence

Sometimes, inappropriate elimination can have the owner at their wits end. Take a second and breathe. If you have done your due diligence in training the companion, then it's time to take a look at medical reasons for why they might be peeing in the house. Some of the top reasons are:

1. Diabetes
2. Bladder stones
3. Tumors

4. Dementia
5. Kidney disease or other kidney failure
6. Urinary tract infections
7. Bladder infections
8. Old Age

Don't punish a dog if they pee in the wrong place, they might need to go to a vet. A veterinarian will help you diagnose a medical problem and guide you with the right medication and methods to fix the problem. Once an animal's medical condition is properly treated and solved, then the inappropriate elimination should stop.

**Successful Potty Training**

There are lots of dos and don'ts when it comes to training our pets, and the same is true for potty training. Many myths exist around the right way to potty train your puppy, and they can do more damage than good.

The first thing is to never punish your puppy for accidents. Punishment at this young of an age, and for something the puppy can't control, can cause a disconnect in your relationship, and the puppy can start to be afraid of you. This is the last thing that you want. It's akin to punishing a baby for using their diaper.

When you see the puppy eliminate in the house, you have two options. You can clap your hands loudly so that the puppy knows to stop and focus on you, or you can ignore their behavior and correct it by replacing it with the behavior you want them to exhibit. Regardless of which route you take, make sure you take the puppy outside and let them finish their business. Once they have successfully eliminated outside, give them a reward or verbal praise.

Sometimes we only find the remnants of an elimination after the fact. In this case you have to clean it up and move on. Never yell at your puppy or spank them for eliminating in the house. Never rub their nose in their mess. None of this will teach the puppy, and it won't understand why it is being punished. Again, reacting negatively can damage your bond with your puppy.

Whenever you have to clean up an accident in the house, make sure that you have an enzyme-based cleaner on hand. Ammonia-based cleaners won't help eliminate the odor. The enzyme-based cleaner will break down the odors in their elimination spot, and prevent them from sniffing the scent and using that same spot again to go potty.

Sometimes your puppy won't go right away when you take them outside. Spend an extra five minutes outside, and give them a chance to do their business. Sometimes, they need some extra time. You'll need to practice patience with your companion.

Try to be consistent with the command that you use to usher them to do their business. Always say the same thing so that the dog gets a chance to recognize the command and the behavior that you want them to perform.

**Crate Training**

Many people use crates to house-train their dogs. The reason for this is that dogs don't like getting their den or bedding area dirty. They like it clean. It's also helpful in a number of other areas. A crate can be a great way to make sure that you control your dog's environment while they are still learning how to become a part of your family.

A word of advice is to not use your crate as a punishment for your dog. It won't solve any problems your dog is exhibiting, and if you misuse the crate, you can leave your dog feeling frustrated or like a trapped animal. This in turn injures your relationship.

If you use the crate to punish your dog, it will have the opposite effect that it is supposed to. You want your dog to go into the crate and not fear it or avoid it.

Dogs need exercise, no matter what kind of breed they are. If you leave your dog cooped up in their crate for prolonged periods, then this can result in a depressed dog. They need to be let out and interact with their humans. There are a few solutions if your schedule doesn't allow you to let your dog out for prolonged periods:

- Change your schedule around to be more accommodating to your dog
- Hire a pet-sitter to come in and let your dog out
- Put your dog in doggy day-care, so they can interact with others and get out of their crate.

If you have a puppy that is younger than six months, then you should keep them in the crate for no more than four hours. They won't be able to control their bladders for very long and inevitably they'll have an accident in their crate.

The crate shouldn't be used as a place to put your dog every time you leave the house. Once you have house-trained your dog well enough that you trust them, you can leave the crate in their area but leave them out. They should choose when they want to go into the crate for the most part. You can use it as their den if you like.

.   .   .

## Choosing the Right Crate

I have already touched a little bit on crate selection, but I'm going to explain a little bit more in-depth now. There are several different options you can use as a crate.

1. **Plastic crates** are the most popular crates purchased. They're easy to transport animals in and if you get the right one you can also use it to house train a dog.

2. **Fabric crates** are the ones that collapse easily for storage. They fold in on each other and are often used for long-distance travel in cars to make it more comfortable for the dog. They're a little difficult to clean sometimes.

3. **Metal crates** are also very common. They collapse down and come apart. Some have dividers to make them bigger and smaller according to your dog's need and growth.

4. **Metal pens.** These can be set up to give a dog a larger area to stretch and roam around in the house. They usually consist of panels that attach to one another to form a circle or square.

When buying your dog's crate, keep in mind the rules of crate sizing:

- The crate should only have enough room for them to stand up in and turn around
- Make sure there is no room for them to potty

Crate training depends on your dog's breed, age, and their personality. Also, you need to factor in what they might have been exposed to in the past when it comes to crates. All those factors can vary the crate training process from a few days to weeks.

## Starting the Crate Training

Crate training happens in steps. You can't jump from step-one to step-five, and wonder why your dog isn't responding the way you expected. Take it slow and let them lead the way. Remember that if you have a solid foundation of trust with your dog this can be easier.

**Step One:** Let your dog meet the crate. You want to put the crate in a central area that you or the whole family will spend a lot of time. Remember that your dog doesn't want to be on its own, it wants you. The best way to do this is to put a blanket or towel in the crate to make it more comfortable, and leave the door open or take it off completely. Then, have your dog in the same room as the crate. Some dogs will explore the crate sooner than others. If you're lucky you'll have a dog that steps into the crate and starts sleeping in it instantly. However, not all dogs act this way.

If you find that your dog isn't taking to the crate as quickly, move towards the crate and speak to them calmly and happily (dogs reflect your energy). Use treats to get your dog to enter the crate and show them that there is nothing to fear.

Sometimes your dog might not want to go all the way into the crate at first. Never push or force them in. Let them decide on their own when the right time is.

**Step Two:** Start giving your companion their food in the crate. Now that your dog has some familiarity, give them their meals next to or in the crate. A dog that isn't fearful of their crate should have their meals placed all the way at the back of the crate.

When you get your dog to stand all the way in the crate with their food bowl, and they exhibit no signs of fear or stress, then you can start closing the door and let them eat their meal. The first time you close the door, make sure you open it right away when you see they've finished eating. This will assure the dog that they're not trapped. Each feeding, let the door stay closed for a few more minutes until they manage to stay comfortably in the crate for 10 or 12 minutes after they're done eating.

**<u>Pro Tip</u>: If they whine while in the crate, don't let them out immediately. Once they stop, then let them out. This way you're not indulging in their negative behaviors.**

**Step Three:** keep doing step two but extend the length of time. When they're happily in the crate, start using the crate outside of feeding times. Use a treat to coax them in, and make sure you're using a consistent command that they can relate to their kennel time.

Use verbal praise when your dog enters the crate, and only give them the treat once they are in the crate. For the first few times, stay next to the crate for a few minutes before going out of the room for a minute. Don't be gone for more than a few minutes, and when you come back stay by the crate for five more minutes before you let them out.

**<u>Pro Tip</u>: Gradually lengthen the times they're in the crate and that you're gone, until they can handle you being gone for 30 minutes while they are in the crate.**

**Step Four:** Coax your dog into the crate when you get ready to go somewhere. When you get ready to leave the house, use a treat or a toy to get them in the crate, accompanied by your command.

When you come home, your dog will most likely be excited. Try your best not to exacerbate their excitement. Keep your voice and energy calm when you get home. This way they won't experience anxiety while excitedly waiting for you to come home.

When they are okay with you leaving for periods throughout the day, start crating your puppy at night. Again, you will use a command and a reward to get them in the crate.

**Pro Tip:** Depending on the anxiety of your dog, move the crate closer to the bed during bedtime so the dog knows you are nearby. The purpose is to get it used to sleeping overnight in the crate.

### Crating Problems and How to Solve Them

Training always has a learning curve, and sometimes problems will pop up. One of the biggest problems pet owners experience is that their dog whines. The cause of overnight whining can be difficult to pinpoint. Is your dog whining because they want to be let out of the crate or because they have to go potty?

If you've been firm in your training and you haven't rewarded them by letting them out of the crate for whining the past, then it is easier to decipher why they are whining. Give them a few minutes. A dog that is testing you will stop whining in a few minutes. Never pound on the crate, throw anything at the crate, or yell at the dog to shut up. This will injure your relationship and most likely increase the whining.

After a few minutes, if your dog is still whining, then you can give the command that signals it's time to go potty.

Watch their reaction. If they get excited by this command, that means they need to go out. Take them out to eliminate. Remember to not let them play in this instance, this trip is to potty, not to play.

If they continue whining, but you know they don't need to potty ignore them. You need to ignore the bad behavior to show them that it doesn't get rewarded.

Separation anxiety is another problem that can occur. Crate training won't fix these issues in your dog. In fact, while it might prevent them from destroying the house, their attempts to get out of the crate and to you, could cause them injury. In this instance you should try <u>desensitization and counter-conditioning techniques.</u>

There are also certain times that are a bad idea to crate your dog. For example:

- If your dog is sick with either vomiting or diarrhea, it is not a good idea to confine them to a crate.
- A dog that hasn't been walked or exercised before being put in a crate.
- When you're gone longer than four hours, with no one to let your dog out.
- If they use the crate to relieve their bowels.
- When a companion doesn't stop barking or whining while in the crate.

**I Can't Crate my Dog**

Not all dogs are suitable to be crated. That's understandable. You have a few options you can use to try to combat leaving your dog alone and uncrated.

1. Hire a dog-sitter or even a dog-walker that can come while you're away and let your dog out to give them exercise.
2. Bring your dog to work with you. More and more workplaces are allowing employees to bring their dogs to work. Of course, you need to check with your boss, and make sure that your dog is properly trained not to bark and whine. You'll want to bring their bed and make their space by your desk or in your office as comfortable as possible.
3. Be aware that not all work spaces are safe for your pet. You want to keep in mind what they have access to and limit this if possible. Electrical cords and purses should be out of their reach.
4. Remember the signs for stress so that you can observe your dog and make sure that they're not stressed by the change in their environment if you take them to work.

However, your dog will need to know basic commands, and obey them so that they don't jump on people, or act in inappropriate ways in the office. Keep reading through this chapter to learn more about those commands.

**Trained Commands**

When taking your dog around other people, especially in a workplace environment, then it is important to make sure that they know a few basic commands like "sit" and "no."

*Sit*

- Stay close to your dog and have a treat in your

hand. If you are clicker training, you will put your clicker in your other hand. Wait for your dog to naturally sit.

- Once they sit, give them verbal praise and throw the treat in their direction. When you give them the treat, make sure it lands far enough away that the dog has to get up to fetch it.
- When they get up, wait until the dog sits again. When the desired behavior is completed, give them praise and another treat. You will probably need to repeat these steps about 12 or so times.
- After the companion understands the behavior, wait for them to sit and include a hand signal to show them when they need to sit.
- When they respond to the hand signal, start training them with the verbal command "sit."
- Keep the training steps up until your dog sits on command every single time.

*Stay*

To get your dogs to learn when to stay in place use the following steps:

- Tell them to sit and then hold your arm out in front of you and have the flat of your palm facing the dog.
- Slowly step back and wait. Keep your palm in front of you. When you walk back give them verbal praise and a treat. Repeat this process until the dog obeys the signal.
- Once they listen to the signal, start using the verbal command "stay."
- Move away a little farther each time you practice

the command. Then, give your dog a treat when they have stayed successfully.

- To make it more challenging, bring in distractions to make sure they follow the command.

### No Barking

Barking can be a little more difficult to correct. Especially in a dog who is accustomed to making noise to get what they want. When trying to correct this behavior, focus on reducing the action instead of eliminating it completely.

When your dog starts to bark, ignore their behavior. Remove them from triggers that will cause them to start making noise as well. When you engage with them when they do, you are teaching them that barking will elicit a response from you.

### Lay Down

To get your dog to lay down, follow these steps:

- Have a treat in your hand and let your dog see it. When they do, place your hand palm down and flat on the floor. The treat should be between your hand and the floor.
- As your dog tries to get the treat they will lay down. The second they lay down, use verbal praise, and let them have the treat.
- Keep repeating this action until they recognize your hand signal as "lay down."
- Add in the verbal command when they have mastered

your hand signal. Use "Down" but be careful not to say it when referring to furniture, or you'll confuse your dog with what you want. When they're on surfaces they shouldn't be on, use the cue "off."

## Come

The "come" command is also known as a recall command. This is one of the most important commands to teach your dog. Try to teach them as early as possible, especially if you adopt a puppy. The older your dog gets, the more independent they get, and the harder the recall command is to teach. I find that this training works best with two people.

- Have one person kneel down on the ground with the puppy or dog close by. Make sure they are sitting.
- Then sit in front of your dog and call them to you by saying their name and following it with "come." Don't add in any other words. Keep it simple.
- You should be sitting close by, so they don't have to run far. When they come to you, give them verbal praise and a treat or toy.
- Repeat it again except add in more distance. Use the command again. When they come to you, repeat the praise and treat.
- This method is best practiced often, so your dog gets a good foundation for the recall.
- When they come to you on command, try practice calling them when you're not in their immediate line of view.

- Once they mastered coming when they can't see you, up the difficulty by adding in distractions.

<u>**Pro-tip:**</u> if your puppy or dog ignores your recalls and runs after a distraction, don't run after them. This makes them think you're playing a game. Start running in the opposite direction to get your companion to follow you instead. This will also enforce the idea that they need to see you in their line of sight whenever they're out.

*No*

Normally, with dog training you ignore the bad behavior and encourage and praise the behavior that you want to see. However, it is still good to teach your dogs to obey the "no" command, and to have an understanding of it.

- Find some dog-training discs. These discs can make an undesirable sound to discourage your dog from a particular behavior.
- You will need treats as well. Put a treat on the floor and let your dog see it. When the dog moves to eat the treat, gently rattle the discs. Take the treat away while rattling the discs. It's important not to yell or say anything to them.
- Do this a few times. Once your dog is no longer startled by the sound of the discs, they will realize that when it rattles they don't get a treat. Repeat it until your dog stops reaching for the treat when the sound of the discs start. They might give you a look of disappointment.
- Have the dog perform a command they know well

like sit, and reward them with a treat. This helps prevent your dog from getting frustrated.

- If you keep repeating this the dog will realize that the disc sounds mean no. Start saying no as you use the disc and, eventually remove the use of the discs and use the simple command no.

## *Off*

To train your dog to get off of things they're not supposed to be on, try this method:

- If you find them on a couch or bed, say the command "off" and call them to you. When they come, give them praise and a treat. Then have them lay down in an appropriate place. Remember to reward them for obeying the down command.
- Repeat this process whenever they are on something they should not be, and soon they will learn where the right place to sit and lay down is.

# CHAPTER 6

# SOCIALIZING WITH THE WORLD

Socialization is very important for any puppy or dog. It teaches your companion how to interact with the world around it. Animals love socializing, it comes to them naturally, but they still need to be exposed to it. When you socialize your companion you are helping him learn how to adjust to a world of people and dogs that extend beyond the barriers of you and your family.

When you socialize your dog they'll experience different places, people, sounds, and animals. All things that they will encounter at some point. It's best and easiest to socialize your dog when they are still puppies. Besides, puppies exposed to others are reported to be happier and healthier than puppies who missed out on important socialization time. The best time to teach your puppy, and introduce them to new things is between the ages of 3 and 4 months.

At three months your puppy's mind is very malleable, and they're only just starting to learn what being a dog means and looks like. Don't rush socialization, not even with puppies, and follow your dog's lead on what they are and are not ready for.

The easiest way to socialize a puppy is to get them enrolled in a doggy daycare. This way they get to meet and play with other dogs. It teaches them how to interact with other people as well. Treats always help this process along.

*Socialization Benefits*

Having a well-socialized dog brings with it a ton of benefits.

1.  A dog who is socialized will be easier to groom. Dogs who lack socialization often display signs of anxiety when they are not around their owners, and this can make them difficult to work with.
2.  They get extra exercise and more playtime because they do well with others. There are more places that you can take your dog, and where they will be fine around other people and animals. You want your dog to get used to the outdoors because it's a whole world for them to play in.
3.  Socialized dogs won't experience fear and anxiety on the same level as dogs that have been poorly socialized. Naturally, dogs are afraid of the unknown. However, at some point they need to learn what the unknown is and how to handle it. If they're introduced to others from a young age (the puppy stage) then they won't hide or be as fearful as an adult dog.
4.  A social dog will fare better at vet exams. They'll be more accustomed to other people and new sights and sounds, so they will be able to adjust better to the vet than dogs who have not been socialized. Your dog's health relies on veterinary care, and it can become stressful on both owner and animal if

the dog is terrified and the vet is unable to properly conduct an examination. This can impact the dog's health.

5. There is a lower risk of running away from home. High-risk for runaways are dogs that experience anxiety and have not been properly socialized. If they encounter something that scares them, they will instinctively run away. Well-socialized dogs will be curious but remain by your side.

6. Travel is easier. They will be accustomed to the car and new environments. This puts less stress on the dog's system and on you. A stressed dog has lowered immunity, and therefore is more at risk for getting sick. Taking your puppy on car rides can help lower their fear and get them used to family trips!

7. Boarding and kenneling is easier, as well. A social dog will be more prepared to let other people take care of him or her. This can become necessary if you take trips where your dog cannot come with you. It ensures that your dog will get the care you need because they're not afraid of letting someone else handle them.

8. Nobody wants an aggressive dog. They're hard to handle and hard to get other people to interact with. Plus, a lot of accidents can occur when your dog is aggressive. Aggression can stem from the fear of the unknown. A dog that has been exposed to different situations will exhibit little to no aggressive behavior, because they were well socialized.

An important thing to keep in mind is that no matter how old your dog grows, socializing them never truly ends. It's something you're constantly doing and it's a good thing for them to be exposed to new people and new dogs. From different floor surfaces to different types of cars and different plants, each new experience is an opportunity for your dog to learn and grow.

# HOW TO SOCIALIZE

When socializing, take your time. Don't force your dog or puppy to tackle situations they're not ready for yet. Positive reinforcement such as treats, toys, and verbal praise go a long way to aiding your pup's socialization. There are two arenas where socialization occurs: at home and out around town.

**Socializing at Home**

- Start with sights and sounds around the house. Have dishwashers running, blenders turned on, and expose them to the sound of the vacuum cleaner. Let them hear and see your hair dryers and other tools and gadgets that might make sounds. Take them into the yard, if you have one, and let them explore under your watch. Let them sniff all the different smells. It's best to do this with a leash on so you can keep them from chewing on anything that might be harmful to them. If you find your dog is afraid of or nervous of anything in particular, try desensitization and counter-conditioning to get them used to the object or sound.

- Have friends come over, and if your dog is becoming a part of a family, make sure that each member interacts with them and plays with them. Let your puppy or dog sniff and explore visitors that come into the home. Make sure you supervise and use any teaching moments they give you. Watch young children as they play with your companion because you don't want them getting fearful if a child is too rough in play.
- You can acclimatize your puppy to different touches and feelings at home. Make sure to gently touch their ears, their paws, their mouth, and their teeth. This makes it easier when a vet goes to examine them because they're already used to the feelings. It can help if you hold their paws and play with their nails gently, as well.

### Socializing in the Big World

<u>Pro Tip:</u> Let your companion lead the pace of all these interactions. Don't rush them, and move slowly when socializing your dog to something new. Some animals can take longer than others to adjust. Always give them good verbal praise and treats when necessary.

1. Make sure that you are there to control the experience. For sights and sounds, give them opportunities to see the world outside. This can include people skating by, or cars passing by the house. It can even be as simple as experiencing other people walking while out on a walk. Your puppy will get a chance to both see and associate

sounds with these new experiences. Exposing them to traffic noises, and even firework noises, can help them manage other sounds they might experience in life. Thunder can also be scary for a dog to experience, so make sure you're there with them, and make the experience a positive one with reinforcements like verbal praise and rewards.

2. Sometimes when traveling, dogs can get anxiety and even throw up from car sickness. Let your dog get used to riding in the car. Take them out for short trips to a corner store or gas station, and use the car to take them to destinations where they get to run and play (after they've been trained well) so they see the car ride as a treat. It can help if you have a crate or harness in the car to protect your dog, so they have a positive and safe experience.

3. Let them experience places that won't be heavily populated with strange dogs at first. This could be coffee shops with outside seating or even your local stores. Enrolling them in a doggy daycare and obedience school are other places where they can safely learn to socialize with other dogs. Avoid dog parks at first, as you cannot control this type of environment or ensure the behavior of other dogs.

**Pro Tip:** As dogs reach the ages of 2-3, they stop enjoying large packs of dogs they've never met. It's best to introduce them to a dog at a time to get them familiar with strange dogs, and to prevent them from feeling overwhelmed

# LOOSE LEASH WALKS

One of the best ways to socialize your dog to the outside world is through walks. However, so often I see owners with dogs that they can't walk because they pull and run, or I see the owner and dog miscommunication on the walk.

Loose leash walks are my favorite method of dog walking because it gives the dog freedom and is safer for both you and your dog. Plus, it's a lot of fun!

You do need to put in commitment to teach your dog how to walk on a leash loosely. Many dogs fall into the habit of pulling on the leash because it gets an owner to take them where they want to go. This is actually an example of rewarding a negative behavior. You don't want your dog to entirely control the walk. So, how do you train your dog to walk on a leash correctly?

*First step:* As you're walking, start practicing in your house. This gives you greater control. Whenever your dog looks at you, reward them with a treat. When you're walking in the outside world, follow eye contact up with a treat as well.

When you do this, your dog's focus goes back to you. If they're watching you, they won't pull against your leash.

**Second step:** When your dog is in the right spot during a walk, use verbal praise and reward them with a treat. This is also a great time to implement clicker training. On a walk, the right spot is normally in the vicinity of your left leg. For some owners it might be their right leg. However, make sure to pick one side, and stick to that side to have uniformity throughout training. Try to phase out treats if you can bit by bit.

**Third step:** Do what is called the canine cha-cha. At certain times on your walk, gently walk backwards. This will let the dog feel some pressure on the leash. When the dog turns and walks back toward you, give them a treat. Do this even when your dog starts to pull ahead on their leash, and wait for them to correct their path. This also instills in them that collar pulls won't give them their way. Never ever jerk the leash or try to use collar corrections when using this method. Be gentle.

**Fourth step:** Make sure that your dog isn't allowed to wander and pull the leash in any direction. Simply stop in place, and then wait for your dog to come back to you. You should stand still — like a tree. When you feel the pressure on the leash relax, this indicates that your dog is correcting their behavior. Give them a treat when they reach your side again to encourage them to stay there.

**Fifth step:** as you're teaching your dog to follow the leash and leave the lease loose, teach them to follow your finger while on walks. For example, if your dog is in the right spot by your left leg, have the leash in your right hand and more treats in the left hand. Then, point with your left hand. The dog will follow your hand and finger because of the treat.

This can become a fun game for them and makes walks more exciting. As the dog catches up to your hand, give them a treat. Most dogs learn this exercise pretty quickly because it's fun and rewarding!

If your dog is pulling hard on the leash during walks, there could be a disconnect in your relationship and connection. Walks are a good way to work on communication with your dog and try to strengthen that bond. Use commands like stay and eye contact to strengthen the connection on a walk.

With a loose leash your dog is given a greater chance to exercise and to develop confidence in themselves and their surroundings. It's also a great way to introduce them to distractions and teach them to remain on task.

Before you do this, make sure all of your dog's ID tags are up to date so that, if something happens, they can easily be traced back to you. Some dogs make a break for it when you're not suspecting it on a loose leash — that's why I recommend practicing at home first.

Once you feel more confident, take your dog to a park where dogs are allowed to be off-leash. These are normally more secure for dogs that decide to run.

# CHAPTER 7

# HANDLING BAD BEHAVIOR

You've picked up this book because you want a well-trained and well-behaved dog. Sometimes, in order to understand a dog's behavior you need to understand how to handle their bad behavior. Some of the most common bad behaviors that owners experience are barking, chewing, biting, inappropriate jumping up and down, jumping, and digging. Often, the issue is that you just don't understand why they are misbehaving, and you are not reading their cues correctly. In this chapter we are going to explore some of the more common misbehaviors and the best way to handle them.

## Barking

All dogs will be vocal at some point, and some barking isn't necessarily a bad thing. In fact, your dog will probably exhibit a range of barking, howling, whining, and other small vocalizations. The problem comes into play when they start to excessively bark. Excessive barking is one of the most common problems experienced by dog owners.

Understanding the intent behind their bark is the first step in correcting this negative behavior. The reasons your dog will bark will be:

- They want attention
- They are bored
- They are giving a warning or alerting you
- They want to play
- They are excited
- They are anxious
- There are other dogs around

When trying to control overabundant barking, teaching your dog commands such as quiet, or teaching them to bark on command, can help. Make sure to remain consistent and to address concerns like anxiety or boredom that could be causing barking. Don't reward the barking, instead, redirect their behavior. For dogs that have anxiety, try using calming treats or pheromone sprays. These can calm their nerves and cause less barking to occur.

## Begging

This is a huge issue for many dog owners. In fact, it can be hard to correct once a dog starts to beg. Let's go back to basics. The simple reasons why dogs beg are:

- They want your food
- They've been fed from the table before

There are a few things to combat this issue. First, never, ever feed your companion from your plate or the table. It doesn't matter how sweetly they look at you, you're reinforcing bad behavior if you feed them this way. Make it clear to the dog with the command "no." If you need to, confine them to a crate or a separate room while meals are happening. Use positive reinforcement training techniques when they do not beg for scraps. This will adjust their behavior around meal times.

## Chasing

All dogs chase. It's a basic instinct instilled in them from birth. They love to chase you, one another, and other animals they see as prey. Chasing, however, can become a problem when your dog darts off never to be seen again. The main reason dogs chase is that it's a basic predatory instinct.

The best way to combat this behavior is to keep your dog leashed when out. Especially while they are in the training phase. Reinforce any fence around your yard so that your companion doesn't have a chance to bolt after a squirrel or bird.

Train the dog to obey the "come" and "no" commands. Recall commands like "come" are vital to prevent a companion from running away or wandering too far away.

**Pro Tip:** Be aware of the dog's triggers. If you know other animals or joggers will trigger them to chase, avoid these situations until the companion is better trained.

## Not Obeying "Come" Command

This can be a tricky one to correct, and my ultimate suggestion will be to go back to basics. The recall command is sincerely important for all dogs to know and obey. Revisit Chapter 4 under trained commands to see how to best train your dog to obey the "come" command. Companions don't follow through with this because:

- They're stubborn
- Might need more training
- They didn't understand the command
- Weren't properly trained at first.

Start by praising your dog whenever they do come to you. This leads back to shaping behavior which I touched on earlier. Even when you're not in a training session, praise the correct behavior to instill a good foundation. Avoid chasing after the dog if they did not listen to the command. Be firm and clear once, then wait for follow through.

**Pro Tip:** If your dog is being obstinate, it is a sign they don't understand you. Tell them to sit, and then go back to basics on recall training. If you keep shouting commands, they will get frustrated. Use positive reinforcement to get them back on track.

## Whining

Whining can be a very annoying behavior. In fact, it can work your last nerve and end up with the owner giving in to whatever the dog wants.

- Dogs whine to communicate a need or want

Keep in mind that your dog's whine is trying to tell you something. However, giving in shows them that this way of communication works and gets them what they want. An owner doesn't want their companion to partake in that behavior.

If your dog begins to whine, ignore them. Leave the room if you need to. This demonstrates that their whining does not get rewarded. Ignore the whining and reward the behavior when they stop.

Always make sure that their needs are taken care of like food and water. Whining can happen during the process of crate training, and it becomes critical to teach them that a whine won't be answered.

Stay strong and keep ignoring the behavior until they stop whining. When they do stop, then reward the silence with positive reinforcement.

**Pro Tip:** Don't join them in whining or make noise when they whine. This only encourages them. If your companion sees they are getting a response from you for whining, they will keep doing it.

## Digging

Dogs love to dig. It's what they do. However, this can cause significant damage to homes and gardens. You might find that some breeds are instinctively driven to dig more than others — like terriers. Generally, you can find out why your dog is digging and correct the behavior by looking at this list:

- They could be anxious or afraid
- They could be bored
- They have could have unburned energy
- It could be part of their basic instincts
- They might be trying to cool off in the hole or seeking comfort
- They might want to bury a bone or toys

- They could try to use digging to escape or get into an area

When you figure out why your dog is digging, it becomes easier for you to eliminate their access or correct and redirect their behavior. For example, if they're digging because they have extra energy, then simply give them more exercise. This will help tire them out and leave them less energy to dig. If your dog is a natural-born digger, try to set an area aside for them where they are allowed to dig. A great idea is to get them a sandbox. Then use simple training methods to redirect your companion to dig in the designated area.

## Chewing

All dogs chew. This is a natural part of how their genes and instincts are set up. You won't get a dog that doesn't chew anything at all. Actually, you want dogs to chew, because it's important. However, an overabundance of chewing can become a serious issue. Chewing is a difficult behavior for some owners to redirect because it can be so destructive. Typically, your dog chews because:

- They are puppies that are teething
- They are bored
- They have too much energy
- They're curious about a new object
- They have anxiety

The best way to tackle a dog that excessively chews is to redirect their behavior. There are a ton of chew toys out on the market that you can buy to keep your chewer busy! Whenever your dog is found chewing on something inappropriate, simply bring their attention to the chew toy and away from what they were chewing. Don't reprimand them. Ignore the negative behavior and condition them to behave in the way you want — in this case, it's chewing on the toy instead.

It does help to keep items you don't want your dog to chew on out of their reach whenever possible. Making sure that your dog gets tired from exercise is a great way to ensure they don't take out their excess energy by chewing on your favorite pair of shoes.

**Separation Anxiety**

This might be surprising to you, but when it comes to behavior problems in dogs, separation anxiety ranks really high. There are several negative behaviors that a dog can adopt when they experience separation anxiety from their owner. These behaviors range from chewing, relieving their bowels inappropriately, barking, and many other destructive behaviors. Keep in mind that some of these behaviors are due to other causes and not anxiety. A dog that is truly experiencing separation anxiety will exhibit these symptoms:

- Start to get anxious when the owner leaves
- Partake in negative behavior between 15 and 30 minutes of owner leaving
- Always wants to be in the owner's space and follows them around
- Always wants to be touching the owner

For extreme cases of anxiety your dog might require medication. Other milder cases can be handled through consistent training and making use of desensitization techniques.

## Inappropriate Elimination

Nobody wants their dog to pee everywhere and at the wrong times. This can cause foul odors in the home and destroy furniture and other precious items. It also can lead to your dog acting inappropriately when out in public spaces. If you find that your dog is always peeing in the wrong places and not responding to training, take them to the vet to make sure there are no medical issues causing this problem. If no medical problems are the issue, then they might be urinating because of:

- Marking territory
- Anxiety
- Improperly house-trained
- Urination due to excitement or submission

Bear in mind that puppies will experience inappropriate elimination. They haven't learned how to control their bladder 100 percent yet, especially puppies younger than 12 weeks. If this becomes a learned behavior, seeking help from a behavior therapist will be your best option to correct the behavior.

## Jumping

Dogs that jump up on people can become a problem. While it is a natural behavior for a dog to exhibit, the bigger they get, the more likely they could hurt someone. And it's an annoying behavior for a dog to exhibit — especially when they are greeting people.

Preventing jumping up and down can be a little more difficult. You'll have to find the method or technique that works best for you and your pup. As difficult as it is, try to refrain from physically correcting them by holding their paws because this can make them think you're playing with them and will reinforce a negative behavior.

When your dog jumps up on you or other people, make sure to ignore the behavior and turn away. In some cases you might even need to walk away. Make no eye contact with the dog, don't reprimand them, and don't touch them. Once your dog relaxes and sits down you can then reward them to reinforce the correct behavior.

## Biting

You don't want your dog to bite and nip you. However, it can become a nasty habit. A puppy often nips and bites as they are learning about their environment. Socialization with their mother at a young age is important because she teaches the puppies to nip gently. However, sometimes teaching bite inhibition falls on an owner's shoulders. You need to identify whether your dog is biting or nipping because of:

- Fear
- Pain
- Protection
- Defense
- Being a predator

You need to ensure you have a strong relationship with your dog, and they are well socialized in order to fight off biting tendencies.

## Aggression

When a dog is aggressive, they display this by snarling, showing their teeth, biting at people, lunging and growling. All dogs can get aggressive and show aggression. Sadly, some dogs are labeled as more aggressive than others, but you need to keep in mind, it often comes down to their background and how they have been raised.

An aggressive dog will become aggressive for the same reasons that they might bite, but it is still a serious issue. You don't want your dog to be aggressive because this impedes their quality of life and heightens the chance of a bad accident happening — especially around young children.

You should first take your dog to the vet if they exhibit aggressive behavior, to make sure there are no health issues that could be causing aggressive behavior. If there are no answers there, your next step will be to consult with a dog trainer and dog behaviorist to help identify and re-train the dog.

# CHAPTER 8

# BONDING WITH YOUR DOG

You should never overlook the importance of solidifying a deep connection and bond with your dog. Sometimes a relationship might need some help from the start, or you might need to repair a broken bond. A good bond with your dog makes training easier on both you and the dog because it heightens their chances of listening to you and obeying your commands.

When your bond is thriving, you know you have earned the respect of your dog. This is the ultimate goal - for you to respect your companion and for them to respect you in return.

How do you know the difference between a strong and weak bond? Well, there are actually a handful of ways to identify if your bond with your dog needs some improving, or if it is as solid as a rock,

A weak bond can occur between you and your dog for a number of reasons. You could be the sweetest and most empathetic person in this world, yet your dog might still have a disconnect with you. Signs that you have a weak bond include:

- Not wanting to play
- Not listening to commands
- Showing indifference when it comes to you or other family members
- Not wanting to be held or touched
- Running away
- Lack of eye contact
- Acting aggressive
- Purposely disobeying commands
- Seemingly lazy
- Depression

A strong bond with your dog will look entirely different from the signs listed above. A dog can't fake an emotional connection, so it's easy to tell when they are being genuine. A dog with a strong bond with their owner will be animated and have a spring in their step. When you're looking out to see if your dog has formed a strong bond with you, look for these signs:

- They want to be near you
- They watch you even when they're not on the leash
- They listen to your commands with no hesitation
- They're focused on you
- They'll look at you often
- They will love being physically handled by you
- They will be able to communicate their wants and needs to you
- They will protect you from danger
- When taught the recall command, the dog will always come to you

Don't freak out if you read this list and realize that you don't have a strong connection with your dog. Sometimes, we all need to put a little extra work in to make our relationships stronger. This can be relationships with humans or dogs. Your dog isn't automatically going to fall in love with every person that pets them.

If you want to improve your relationship and bond with your dog, you need to consider the way that you act towards them and around them. Even though a fair majority of human-to-human communication is non-verbal, we still like to verbalize our wants, needs, and desires. A dog doesn't understand that verbalization. They communicate through their body language with us. We need to make sure that our non-verbal language is communicating the same thing to our dogs and not overstepping their boundaries. Let's have a look at the ways we can communicate better with our dogs.

Commands can be a big source of frustration between dog and owner. Your dog will understand simple commands, but when you start adding strings of words together, the command gets lost. Sometimes your body language won't match up with the command you're giving, and the number of words you're using confuses the dog. I suggest trying to practice non-verbal cues with your dog. For a whole day, try not to verbalize your affection or needs to them. Use your body to respond to your dog, and see how they interpret your non-verbal cues. You'll be surprised by how much you're saying when you're not talking.

I know we all love to wrap our arms around our dogs and squish them towards us for a hug. Not all dogs love this. Dogs don't hug one another. In the dog world, a dog putting their paw on another dog is showing dominance and control - not affection. Gauge your dog's reaction to see if they're receptive to your hug, or if you're actually making them uncomfortable.

How would you feel if someone had their hands in your face all the time or was patting you on the head? You probably wouldn't like it. Odds are that your dog isn't too fond of having constant pats on the head either. I suggest showing your love and affection with scratches around the neck and under the chin. This gives your dog the opportunity to move away when they're ready to.

This is going to be a tough one for many dog owners out there, but it needs to be said. Forcing your dog to give you "kisses" in the form of licks is actually you trying to force your dominance on your dog. When a dog uses their tongue to lick, they're doing it as a sign of submission. Naturally, dogs do use their tongues to greet and groom their family members, however, there's a difference between asking for the kisses and letting your dog naturally lick you. It's best to let it happen naturally so that your dog can choose what they want to do.

Dogs love to be picked up sometimes, especially depending on their bond with the owner. However, you should not pick them up and hold them like you would a baby. When a dog is high in the air and their backs are towards the grounds it can trigger anxiety. Remember to look out for their body language and what they're telling you.

A dog that is familiar and content with you will be able to maintain eye contact with you. When you approach your dog, make sure that your body isn't towering over them and use a gentle voice. Keep your eyes a little averted at first so the dog understands you don't mean to hurt them. This will help your dog feel secure with you and choose to maintain eye contact.

Dogs love their routine. Contrary to how they act, they actually want and need rules. Rules make your dog's life predictable, comfortable, and a much easier life to navigate. If you're clear about your boundaries, and you're consistent with enforcing them and training your dog, then they'll thrive in the environment that you've set up for them.

Never force your companion to play with people, animals, and other dogs that they're telling you they don't like. Dogs have some people and animals that they prefer to be around and some that they don't like - the same as you in your friend group. If you push your dog to interact in a situation they don't want to, then you're risking an aggressive bite coming out.

You might think that walks are a great way to bond with your companion - and they are! However, are you doing more damage than good on your walks? Your dog is an explorer. They want to sniff, smell, and pee on that tree. When you take them on walks, this is what they're going to want to do. Quick walks where you restrict them from exploring can harm your relationship with them. A dog's sense of smell is their way of seeing the world, in the same way that our eyes are a human's way of seeing the world.

A tight leash can be to you and your companion's detriment. You communicate your body language through your leash. A tight leash can frustrate and even stress your dog. Read up in this guide on how to loose-leash walk your dog safely.

Teasing your dog isn't funny and doesn't help your relationship with them. Teasing can be barking back at a dog, trying to talk to or wave at your dog if they're behind windows or doors. Pulling on a dog's tail or ears. There's a wide list of things we do in jest, that aren't actually funny because they frustrate our companions.

If you are going to dress your dog up in clothes, make sure that they are comfortable with the clothes first. Forcing your dog into clothes that they don't want to be in can hurt your bond. Some dogs love wearing sweaters, hats, and other fun wardrobe items. It's up to you to make sure your dog is content when playing with them in this way.

Sometimes, it is unavoidable to have your dog in strange scenarios. For example, when you take them to the vet. Whenever possible, try to avoid making your dog face a scary situation. If it's unavoidable, take treats along to help with positive reinforcement.

A dog's sense of smell is estimated to be between 100,000 and 100 million times stronger than ours. Think about the scents you put on before you play with your dog. A heavy dab of cologne might not be great for their sensitive noses.

If your dog spends too much of their time alone, then this can injure the way they respond to you. You can break up alone time by enrolling your dog in a doggy daycare or even have a dog walker come in to interact with them.

Puppies see you leaning over them as a way to illustrate you have control. When you're interacting with your puppy, try to do it from the side or while kneeling. It can affect your bond if they see you as attempting to assert dominance by hovering on top of them.

One of the biggest things you can do to rescue a broken bond and to foster a new bond to grow, is to stay calm in the face of your companion. If you're yelling at them this could scare them. Even if you're yelling at someone else in their vicinity or throwing things, your dog feeds off of that energy, and it can leave them terrified. Speak to your dogs in soft voices as much as possible - even when they engage in behaviors you don't want them to repeat. A dog will never understand you yelling at them, so it won't help them learn, or improve your relationship with them.

# CHAPTER 9
# YOUR DOG'S HEALTH

You need to know everything you can about your dog and their health so that you can best facilitate them when they are sick. A sick dog might act out with negative behaviors. If you know when your dog is sick, it makes it easier to identify the reason behind some of their negative behaviors.

The first step towards helping your dog with their health is to make sure that they have a good veterinarian. Always check out a vet's website first. This will show you who their staff is and the kind of environment they foster. You can also find out more about their services and how ready they are to handle emergency situations.

Preferably, you will want your vet to be accredited by the American Animal Hospital Association (AAHA). This is normally identified on their website, but you can also call and ask them.

Sometimes the best way to get a good vet is to ask the community around you for recommendations. Social media platforms are great for this, and you can read reviews on review sites for these veterinarians. It's important to choose the right fit for you and your dog.

Make sure that you familiarize yourself with the clinic schedule. When do they open? How do they bill? This allows you to learn about the clinic, but also gives you a chance to interact with staff members and see how they respond.

You can meet the vets and see how they operate. Is the clinic clean and well-run? Do you feel confident with the number of people on staff to look after your companion?

You also want the vet to be in a location that is easy for you and your dog to get to - especially during emergency situations.

A dog's first appointment with a vet is an opportunity for you to ask the vet and their staff the necessary questions you need answered. You'll also get a closer look at how they run things and if they're organized. Make sure you get along with the vet and communication is clear. When it comes to your dog's health, communication is important.

Some dogs have special needs. This might require you to find a vet that specializes in your dog's condition.

You also want to make sure that the vet you are seeing supports both alternative treatments and cutting edge medical treatments. The solution to your dog's symptoms aren't always pills and drugs, sometimes a holistic approach is helpful for their condition as well, and improves their quality of life.

It can be overwhelming to keep track of all the questions and information you are taking in when visiting a new vet. Take a pen and paper with you if you need to write it down, but here are some important questions you should be asking:

- Are the veterinary technicians on staff licensed?
- How do they handle emergencies?
- How do they monitor overnight patients?
- What medical equipment do they use?
- Do the dogs get referred to specialists?
- How are the animals checked before they have surgery or get anesthesia?
- How does the staff handle pain management cases?
- Do they do diagnostic tests in-house or send them out to a lab?
- Do they have payment plans?
- What payment methods do they accept?

## Vaccinations

Your dog or puppy will need vaccines to help their immune system fight off organisms that bring disease and pain. The vaccines have antigens that mimic the most detrimental disease organisms, however, they don't cause your dog to experience the disease. The vaccine stimulates the immune system and causes it to recognize what to fight off when it's exposed to the real and active disease.

The main vaccines that your dog should be getting, as outlined by the AAHA are:

- Canine Distemper
- Canine Parvovirus
- Rabies
- Hepatitis

There are some vaccines that are not standard or a main vaccine, and are optional for your dog to get. Keep in mind that some boarding and doggy day care facilities might require these vaccines:

- Canine Influenza
- Lyme Vaccine
- Bordetella
- Leptospirosis

Most states require that your dog is up-to-date on their rabies vaccination. Make sure you read up on your state laws regarding dog vaccinations to make sure that you are in compliance.

Discuss vaccinations with your vet to make sure that your companion is getting the right immunizations. Some dogs don't need all the vaccines, depending on their age, environment, and medical history.

If you have a new puppy, the first set of vaccines are normally administered when they are between 6 and 10 weeks old. It's imperative you keep up with your puppy's vaccination schedule to give them the best chance at life.

As your puppy matures into a dog, their vaccines turn into boosters that simply help boost their system against the diseases they could be susceptible to. They are typically boosted around one year. Some vaccines like Rabies can last for three years before they are needed again - consult your vet about this.

Your dog's vaccines will last approximately:

- Rabies — 3 years
- DHPP — 3 years

- Bordetella — 6 months
- Lyme Disease — 1 year
- Canine Influenza — 1 year
- Leptospirosis — 1 year

Vaccine benefits are above and beyond any risk that might be experienced, and while bad reactions to vaccines are rare, it is important to watch your dog and know what symptoms to look out for in case they do react badly. Symptoms to watch out for 24-48 hours after a vaccine are:

- Loss of appetite
- Lethargy
- Fever
- Swelling in paws or face
- Diarrhea
- Vomiting
- Swelling by vaccine area
- Seizures or difficulty breathing (anaphylactic shock)

If your dog's symptoms are mild, monitor them and make sure they improve. If a reaction is severe, call your veterinarian immediately and follow their instructions.

**Doggy Health Care**

*Spaying and Neutering*

Your priority will be your dog's overall health care. Spaying or neutering your dog falls into health care. Dogs that are sterilized experience healthier lives and live longer than those who aren't. It's also part of being a responsible dog owner because it prevents the overpopulation of puppies and dogs who go without homes.

### *Vitamins*

Like humans, dogs need vitamins too. Most dogs get their vitamins through their diet as their food is especially formulated for their needs. However, you might find that your dog is lacking vitamins and nutrients. It's important to know what your dog needs and how much, so that you can more accurately discuss this with your dog's vet.

Dog's need vitamin A for their growth, immune function, and the function of their cells.

B vitamins are essential for your dog. They include thiamine, riboflavin, niacin, B12 and B6. These vitamins aid with energy and metabolism, enzyme function, and red blood cell function. B6 also helps with glucose production, regulation of hormones, and gene activation. Pantothenic acid (B5) helps your dog to metabolize nutrients, and folic acid helps with metabolizing amino acids, and plays a role in protein synthesis in the cell.

Vitamin C gives your dog the antioxidants they can use to prevent inflammation. Fun fact: a dog's liver makes and produces vitamin C on their own, unlike ours, and they do not require vitamin C consumption to prevent illness.

Vitamin D helps your dog balance minerals, such as calcium, for the growth and development of their bones. Check with your vet before augmenting their diet with vitamin D as it can build up and cause problems.

Your dog also needs vitamin E. This vitamin is fat-soluble and helps with both cell function and your dog's metabolism of fat. It is best to check with your vet regarding any fat-soluble vitamin as they can build up in the body if they are overdone.

Vitamin K helps your dog's blood clot. If your dog has accidentally swallowed a poison, it can reduce their levels of vitamin K and impede the function of blood clotting which can lead to hemorrhaging.

Your dog's phospholipid cell membranes need choline in their makeup. Choline helps with liver function, brain function, and can also be used to treat dogs with epilepsy.

Since your dog's food and diet should cater and account for all the vitamins and nutrients they need, it's not often necessary to supplement them. However, depending on your companion's health and age, your vet might recommend a supplement for them. Always consult with your vet before giving your dog a supplement or drastically changing their diet because a lack of or overabundance of vitamins can impact their health. For example, an influx of vitamin A can give your dog joint pain and make them dehydrated.

*Is My Dog Healthy?*

It can be easy to pinpoint if your dog is healthy and thriving under your care - you simply need to pay attention to their signs.

Fresh breath is a sign of good health in a dog. Gum disease and tooth decay can indicate a problem with your dog's health, and a rotting smell coming from their mouth is an easy way to check this. Make sure you brush your dog's teeth regularly, to help prevent this.

If your dog's coat is shiny and clean (barring their rolls in the mud) then that's a positive sign of a healthy dog. If you find that your dog is losing hair or scratching a lot it could be a sign they have an allergy or other condition.

A good lean weight on your dog is the best sign that they are eating right and getting the right amount of exercise. Many vets are concerned about pet obesity, as this can have detrimental effects on the overall health of your companion.

If your dog is going to the bathroom on a regular basis, then this is a good sign of health. Checking your dog's bowel movements can tell you a lot about their health. You don't want their poop to have any worms, diarrhea, mucus, or blood. Transparent yellow pee is a good sign on health as well.

A dog that shows engagement and is alert and interested in the world around them, is a dog in good health.

Check your dog's ears, they often go overlooked by owners. You want your dog's ears to be clean and free of any odors. If you smell a bad odor coming from your dog's ears take them to the vet. Regular ear cleaning can help prevent smelly ears and infections.

Use this checklist to make sure you're keeping up with your dog's overall health:

- Vet checks once a year (twice a year for senior dogs)
- Daily exercise
- Staying inside to regulate their temperature from being too hot or too cold
- Brushing their teeth 3-5 times a week
- Keeping them hydrated
- Grooming them
- Regulating their diets

## Common Health Problems

The odds are that during your pet's lifetime they will have a few issues that crop up. Here are some of the most common issues:

1. Skin issues are at the top of the list. If your dog is scratching himself a lot, or their skin looks irritated, it's a sign of a problem. You might see the skin get inflamed, red, scaly, or flaky. The reason for this can range from an allergy to a parasite, and veterinary care should be sought.
2. Urinary tract infections (UTIs). A sign of a UTI could be a dog that is eliminating in the house even though they are house-trained. If your dog is urinating excessively, drinking a lot, or has bloody urine take them to the vet for a check.
3. Parasites can be external like ticks, or internal like worms. If you use a preventive topical treatment you can normally avoid your dog getting ticks or fleas. There are also medications available to prevent or treat worms.
4. Obesity is a common health problem that leads to a wide variety of other health problems. Make sure you're monitoring your dog's diet and exercise to make sure that they're not overeating.
5. Arthritis. Dogs get arthritis too, and it can cause pain and inflammation in their joints. If you think your dog might have arthritis, consult your vet. They'll have supplements to help your dog's joints and other medications to help prevent the disease from worsening.

*Keeping Vet Costs Low*

Sometimes, it is unavoidable and you're hit with a hefty vet bill for your dog's medical care. There are a few ways to combat this.

My first suggestion is to get pet health insurance if you can. There are a ton of companies that sell pet insurance, and you can shop around for the one that meets your needs and budget the best. This can help offset really high vet bills.

Some vets allow you to trade goods and services for payment of their treatment. Speak to your vet to see what options are viable for you.

Always let your vet know what your financial situation is. They can come up with options and resources for you to use. It also ensures they'll try to go the least expensive route to help you and your companion.

Before any services are done, always have your vet give you a written estimate for what they plan on doing to your dog. This allows you to go in to any treatments knowing exactly what needs to be done and how much it will cost.

Medications and supplements can be expensive. Shop around at different pet stores and online pet stores to get the best price possible on their medicine.

# AFTERWORD

This guide has taken you from bringing your dog home and making a safe space in their new environment, to what you need to know about their health and their care. Hopefully, every question that you had when you picked up this book has been answered with some clarity.

You have learned the importance of bonding with your companion and creating a relationship with them, before you start training them. You've also learned how you might be damaging your relationship with your dog without being aware.

By now, your understanding of your dog should be on a different level to when you read the introduction. I'm confident that if you follow the methods and techniques in this book, you will have both a well-trained and well-behaved dog. Especially if you have learned to read their body language and what they are communicating to you.

Now, you should have the power and the knowledge to combat your dog's negative behaviors and turn your dog into a cohesive unit of the family!

I want to thank you for choosing this guide to help you fit your new companion into your home. If you've found that this book has helped you and your dog, then I hope you would be so kind as to leave a review for the book so that other owners can help bond with their dogs the same way you have.

# REFERENCES

ASPCA. (2015). *People Foods to Avoid Feeding Your Pets.* ASPCA. https://www.aspca.org/pet-care/animal-poison-control/people-foods-avoid-feeding-your-pets

ASPCA. (2017, June 21). *7 Tips on Canine Body Language.* ASPCA Professional; ASPCA. https://www.aspcapro.org/resource/7-tips-canine-body-language

Best Friends Behavior Consultants. (2020). *Relationship-Based Dog Training: Benefits.* Best Friends Animal Society. https://resources.bestfriends.org/article/relationship-based-dog-training-benefits

Burke, A. (2017, May 24). *7 Vitamins Your Dog Needs for a Healthy Lifestyle.* American Kennel Club; American Kennel Club. https://www.akc.org/expert-advice/nutrition/vitamins-dogs-need-healthy-lifestyle/

Clark, M. (2019, January 10). *7 Most Popular Dog Training Methods - Dogtime.* Dogtime. https://dogtime.com/reference/dog-training/50743-7-popular-dog-training-methods

Coren, S. (2000). *How To Read Your Dog's Body Language.* Modern Dog Magazine. https://moderndogmagazine.com/articles/how-read-your-dogs-body-language/415

Dogtopia. (2018, August 14). *Bonding With Your Dog - Are You Straining the Relationship?* Edmond. https://www.dogtopia.com/edmond/bonding-with-your-dog/

Flowers, A. (2020, June 14). *Tips for House training Your Puppy.* WebMD. https://pets.webmd.com/dogs/guide/house-training-your-puppy#2

Fratt, K. (2004). *Reward-Based Training Versus Punishment: Which is Better? | Journey Dog Training.* Journeydogtraining.Com. https://journeydogtraining.com/reward-based-training-versus-punishment-which-is-better/

Georgia Veterinary Associates. (2016, July 28). *Dog Vaccinations.* Georgia Veterinary Associates. https://www.mygavet.com/services/dogs/dog-vaccinations

Lee, C. (2019, October 28). *Top 5 Steps To Take When Choosing A Good Vet.* Dogtime. https://dogtime.com/dog-health/general/19482-top-5-steps-to-choosing-a-good-vet

Millan, C. (2019, July 18). *Well Trained But Not Well Behaved.* Cesar's Way. https://www.cesarsway.com/well-trained-but-not-well-behaved/

Nicholas, J. (2017, March 17). *10 Point Checklist for Puppy Proofing Your Home.* www.Preventivevet.com. https://www.preventivevet.com/dogs/checklist-for-puppy-proofing-your-home

PawCastle. (2017, July 10). *7 Surprising Reasons Why Dog Socialization Is Important.* Paw Castle. https://pawcastle.com/why-dog-socialization-is-important/

Purina. (2020). *Basic Dog Training Commands*. Purina; Purina. https://www.purina.co.uk/dogs/behaviour-and-train-ing/training-your-dog/basic-commands-for-your-dog

Stregoswki, J. (2019, October 31). *10 Common Dog Health Problems You Should Know*. The Spruce Pets. https://www.thes-prucepets.com/common-dog-health-problems-1117863

Sullivan, K. (2019, January 2). *The Dos and Don'ts of Grooming Your Dog at Home | PETA*. PETA. https://www.peta.org/living/animal-companions/dogs-home-grooming/

The Humane Society. (2018). *Crate training 101*. The Humane Society of the United States. https://www.humanesoci-ety.org/resources/crate-training-101

Toll Brothers. (2018, November 5). *5 Ways to Create a Special Space for Your Pet*. Build Beautiful. https://www.tollbrothers.-com/blog/create-a-space-for-your-pet/

CPSIA information can be obtained
at www.ICGtesting.com
Printed in the USA
LVHW010619051020
667928LV00005B/415